CAMBRIDGE LIBRARY COLLECTION

Books of enduring scholarly value

History

The books reissued in this series include accounts of historical events and movements by eye-witnesses and contemporaries, as well as landmark studies that assembled significant source materials or developed new historiographical methods. The series includes work in social, political and military history on a wide range of periods and regions, giving modern scholars ready access to influential publications of the past.

On the Use and Abuse of Literary and Ecclesiastical Endowments

Scottish minister and social reformer Thomas Chalmers (1780–1847) is famous as the leader of the group of 470 ministers who left the Church of Scotland in 1843 to found the Free Church of Scotland, and as the author (in 1834) of the first Bridgewater Treatise (also reissued in this collection). Along with his theological interests, Chalmers was deeply concerned with educational reform in schools and universities. In 1827 he published this paper on university endowments, asserting that it was the state's responsibility to support religious and educational institutions, because churches, schools, and universities maintained the nation's Christian principles and character. Chalmers argued that only endowed national establishments were capable of ensuring the religious and moral well-being of the individual. In addition to his appeal for university endowments, he also advocated (unusually for his time) the extension of full civil rights to dissenters and Catholics.

Cambridge University Press has long been a pioneer in the reissuing of out-of-print titles from its own backlist, producing digital reprints of books that are still sought after by scholars and students but could not be reprinted economically using traditional technology. The Cambridge Library Collection extends this activity to a wider range of books which are still of importance to researchers and professionals, either for the source material they contain, or as landmarks in the history of their academic discipline.

Drawing from the world-renowned collections in the Cambridge University Library, and guided by the advice of experts in each subject area, Cambridge University Press is using state-of-the-art scanning machines in its own Printing House to capture the content of each book selected for inclusion. The files are processed to give a consistently clear, crisp image, and the books finished to the high quality standard for which the Press is recognised around the world. The latest print-on-demand technology ensures that the books will remain available indefinitely, and that orders for single or multiple copies can quickly be supplied.

The Cambridge Library Collection will bring back to life books of enduring scholarly value (including out-of-copyright works originally issued by other publishers) across a wide range of disciplines in the humanities and social sciences and in science and technology.

On the Use and Abuse of Literary and Ecclesiastical Endowments

CAMBRIDGE UNIVERSITY PRESS

Cambridge, New York, Melbourne, Madrid, Cape Town,
Singapore, São Paolo, Delhi, Tokyo, Mexico City

Published in the United States of America by Cambridge University Press, New York

www.cambridge.org
Information on this title: www.cambridge.org/9781108036672

© in this compilation Cambridge University Press 2011

This edition first published 1827
This digitally printed version 2011

ISBN 978-1-108-03667-2 Paperback

ON ENDOWMENTS.

ON THE

USE AND ABUSE

OF

LITERARY AND ECCLESIASTICAL

ENDOWMENTS.

BY

THOMAS CHALMERS, D. D.

PROFESSOR OF MORAL PHILOSOPHY IN THE UNIVERSITY OF ST. ANDREWS.

———

GLASGOW:

PRINTED FOR WILLIAM COLLINS;

WILLIAM WHYTE & CO. AND WM. OLIPHANT, EDINBURGH;
R. M. TIMS, AND WM. CURRY, JUN. & CO. DUBLIN;
AND G. B. WHITTAKER, LONDON.

1827.

Printed by W. Collins & Co.
Glasgow.

PREFACE.

———

WHEN a teacher, whether of Christianity or of science, derives all his remuneration from the fees of those who attend him; and when he is further enabled, by these fees, to uphold the fabric in which the work of his vocation is carried on, it may be thought that he stands wholly apart from the aid of endowments. The term most generally suggests the idea of a salary, and sometimes, perhaps, there may be included in it, the idea of an erection. A school, for example, may be endowed only to the extent of its architecture; or, additionally to this, it may be endowed to the further extent either of a partial or total income to the teacher. Each of these is included in our idea of an endowment; for, in whatever shape the aid be rendered, whether in that of a gratuitous building, or of a gratuitous revenue, if it form no part of the price given for education by those who have a spontaneous demand for it, then, according to the use made of the word in the following pages, it comes under the head or character of an endowment.

But our argument leads us to employ the term in a meaning still more comprehensive. Our endeavour is, to estimate the effect of all that support which is given to education, over and above the recompense afforded to it in fees, by those who have a *spontaneous* demand for it. This recompense is found to be enough in the case of all those free marketable commodities which form the great subjects of supply on the one hand, and of demand on the other. The demand calls forth the supply. It is so willing a demand, that the price it offers draws out the supply; and the supply finds, in the price thus offered, its adequate and its whole remuneration. It is not so with the supply of education, in those cases where the teacher is paid in part or in whole, or where a seminary is provided for him, or a dwelling-house built, or an apparatus purchased and kept in repair, or a library collected and maintained, or any fraction,

in short, of the requisite equipment upheld by a
fund otherwise constituted than from the fees of
the scholars. Each and all of these auxiliary do-
natives are so many endowments. But there are
cases, when the scholars' fees, the price paid by
them for education, might prove to be sufficient
for all the purposes now specified; and yet, from
the law and nature of their attendance, the greater
part, if not the whole, of these fees may have the
very effect on learning, whether beneficial or mis-
chievous, which the gratuities conferred upon it
have had; and which may, therefore, well be put
down to the account of endowments.

We would, therefore, further regard that as an
endowed seminary, attendance upon whose courses
of instruction was made a requisite condition for
the subsequent holding of any lucrative offices.
It is thus that an attendance is obtained for colleges, greatly beyond the spontaneous demand for
that education which they furnish. For example,
a course of logic at one or other of our universities, is a pre-requisite to the admission of our students into the divinity hall, and therefore to their
admission into orders, so as to be qualified for presentation to a church living. There can be no

doubt, that the classes of logic are indebted to this regulation for many of their students; and the same holds true of all the other classes which enter into the curriculum of the theological profession. This is what Dr. Smith denominates, and indeed stigmatizes as a " statute of apprenticeship;" and what he argues against, on the same grounds that he does against the corporation laws, and the compulsory terms of preparation for any of the trades or callings in ordinary artizanship. The other learned professions, as law and medicine, have also their statutes of apprenticeship, inasmuch as certain university classes must be attended by those who are admitted as licentiates in either of these professions. Now, every class which derives benefit from such a regulation, we hold to be, to the extent of that benefit, an endowed class. The augmentation of revenue which accrues therefrom, comes, no doubt, to the professor, in the shape of fees; but it is as little due to the spontaneous demand for his instructions, as if it had come to him in the shape of salary. It has all the virtue, or, as Smith would have it, all the vice of an endowment. As such, therefore, we regard it; and it being our single object to contrast that system, under which education is wholly paid for by those who attend spontaneously upon its lessons, with that other system under which the remuneration is helped out from other sources, and by other expedients, we scarcely notice a distinction in our general argument be-tween salaries and statutes of apprenticeship.

It is further obvious, that, in this view, bursaries have the same character and effect with other en-dowments. They draw a greater number of stu-dents to the higher seminaries of education than would otherwise attend them. They go to aug-ment the income of the teacher beyond what he would enjoy, were scholarship, like an article of ordinary merchandise, left to the pure operation of demand and supply, unfostered by bounties, and unforced by compulsory enactments. Our main inquiry is, in how far education should be so left, or whether it has not been both sublimed in its character, and increased in amount, by those artificial encouragements which our forefathers have annexed to it.

Certain it is, that somewhat of an adverse feel-ing to these encouragements, has been generated by the reigning taste and philosophy of our times.

We are now quite familiarized to the discovery, that in commerce there has been a cumbrous excess of legislation, and from which, when delivered, it regains the healthful play of nature and liberty. And the same principle which has been verified both by experience and reasoning, in the business of ordinary trade, has also been applied to the business of education. The bounties, in particular, which have been demonstrated to be so hurtful to the one, are vaguely imagined to be alike hurtful to the other. And so it is conceived, that scholarship will best thrive, when placed in the circumstances in which it is now found that merchandise best thrives; that is, when let alone, or when, relieved both from the fetters and from the encouragements which have been laid upon it by the state, it is entirely upholden by the demand of society, and by the price which society is willing to give for its lessons.

Dr. Smith was the first who proclaimed these principles—and not without effect, we apprehend, on the legislators both of this and of other countries. During the anarchy of the French Revolution, the schools and establishments for medical education were suspended, and their places supplied by a few irregular lectures given by individuals. The inconvenience of this, was repaired by the Convention, impelled to the re-endowment of colleges and classes, by the pressing wants of the army for a competent supply of properly educated surgeons. But while government kept up the higher schools, they neglected the schools of general education ; and the system of allowing them to increase or diminish according to the abilities or inclination of individuals, was defended on the authority of Smith.*

In our own country, that authority is now more deferred to, than it wont to be, on all the proper subjects of political economy. At the interval of half a century, the speculations of this great author have been incorporated in the practices of government. This is the time which truth and wisdom have taken to travel from the philosopher's study to the senate-house ; and at length, after having struggled its way through many obstructions, the

---

* The information of this paragraph, is extracted from the valuable work of Dr. Johnston, entitled, " A General View of the Present System of Public Education in France."—See this interesting narrative, which begins at page 103, of his volume.

system of free trade is not only recognized, but is begun to be acted on in the regulation of commercial affairs. It is precisely at such a season; and in the recency of an author's triumphs, that we should expect the ascendancy of his errors as well as of his sounder and better principles. And accordingly, we think we can perceive both in and out of Parliament, a certain impression that education should be left to itself, just as trade should be left to itself—so that, as in the one case, the remuneration should lie wholly in the market-price, unhelped by a bounty, in the other, the remuneration should lie wholly in the fees unhelped by a salary. The compulsory attendance on certain classes of the students who are in the course of preparation for the learned professions, comes under the like condemnation of a liberal philosophy. Altogether the principle is adverse to our established church, and to our established colleges— and in the " Wealth of Nations" there are passages of great force and celebrity which are adverse to both.*

The object of the following work, is to estimate

---

* See Note A, Appendix.

the soundness of this economic principle as applied
to education, unexceptionable though it may be in
its application to the affairs of merchandise. It
is not for the mere sake of rectifying a naked
position in economical science that this work has
been undertaken—for it will be found that the
question, both of religious and literary establishments, is involved in the discussion—and that the
argument thence educed in their favour, which at
least appears a very strong one to ourselves, has
this further claim to attention, that it has not been
commonly insisted on.

We should have gone more into detail on the
methods and constitution of colleges, had not the
practical necessity of this been superseded by the
appointment of a Royal Commission on the Universities of Scotland, whose inquiries, there is every
reason to believe, will terminate in a result alike
honourable to its members, and satisfactory to the
public at large. We shall have succeeded in our
aim, if, by this humble contribution to the aggregate
of information and testimony drawn from so many
individuals, we shall have at all helped to soften
the prejudice which obtains against the holders of
literary and ecclesiastical benefices, or to reconcile

the community to a more generous system of endowments, as being at once accordant with the soundest lessons of philosophy, and subservient to the best and the purest objects of patriotism.

CONTENTS.

———

CHAP. I.

CHAP. II.

CHAP. III.

CHAP. IV.

APPENDIX.

USE AND ABUSE

OF

LITERARY AND ECCLESIASTICAL

ENDOWMENTS.

———

CHAP. I.

GENERAL ARGUMENT IN FAVOUR OF ENDOWMENTS.

1. It has not been found necessary to endow an establishment for supplying a population with any of the articles of ordinary merchandize. We have not, for example, a national establishment of bakers, or tailors, or masons, as we have of school-masters, professors, and clergymen. And the reason is quite obvious why the former kind of establishment is uncalled for. The physical wants or appetites of our nature guarantee an effective demand for the various articles of physical indulgence. Rather than want food, or clothes, or lodging, man will exert himself to the uttermost, that, either by his labour, or the price of his labour, he may be enabled to purchase these indispensable

B

accommodations. They whose office it is to provide such accommodations, do not need to be remunerated by the State for their services; for, in the price which customers are willing to give rather than want them, they find a sufficient remuneration. It is thus that the providing of a nation with what may be termed the physical necessaries of life, may be safely confided to the spontaneous operation of the principle of demand and supply. It is in fact a self-regulating interest, and should, in as far as government is concerned, be simply let alone.

2. The same is true of what may farther be termed the common, or the physical luxuries of life. For these the vanity and the sensuality of man together, will secure a sufficiently energetic demand, on the part of all who can afford to purchase them. There is no danger lest, up to the measure of their wealth, men will not be induced to expend enough for the higher gratifications of appetite; or that, rather than want them, they will not afford a full remunerating price for the various articles of parade and luxury. The tradesmen, or the merchants who provide these articles, do not need to have their recompense helped out by Government; for they can find a full recompense in the wealth and good-will of their own customers. And, even should there not be the will along with the wealth, there is no national interest at all hurt or put to hazard, although so many of the affluent

of our land should choose to live penuriously, or to abridge the style and splendour of their establishments. At least, it does not seem to be any object of national policy, to stimulate, by public encouragement, and at the public expense, the supply of luxuries beyond what is called for by the native demand and disposition of the people themselves. This, too, therefore, is treated by Government as a self-regulating interest; and, as such, is also let alone.

3. It is this principle of letting things alone which, a truly wise and beneficent principle in its application to all the articles of ordinary merchandize, forms the essence of the philosophy of free trade. In general commerce, the two elements of demand and supply should be left to balance each other, and to find their own proper adjustment. The hand of legislation, when it intermeddles with this mechanism, only deranges it; and, whether it does so by its artificial restrictions, or its artificial bounties, it is sure to lessen and to retard the prosperity of a nation. There is no patriotic interest served by the commodities of ordinary trade being multiplyed beyond what the people of the land are both willing to use, and able to pay for. It is thus that an endowment in behalf of the wine trade, or the tobacco trade, or the sugar trade, or, which is the same thing, the annexation of a bounty either to the production or the importation of these articles, would, in

these days, be deemed an outrage on all the maxims of a sound political economy. It would rank among the senilities of a darker age, which are now exploded, and have long gone by—alike disowned by the present generation of statesmen, and revolting to the liberal and enlightened spirit of our modern science.

4. Now, this principle, of such undoubted truth and value in its application to the business of trade, has also been applied to the business of education. The same exceptions have been taken against an endowment in behalf of learning, which are now taken, by every sound economist, against a bounty. It is held to be an interference with the free operation of that demand, to which it is imagined that the whole supply of a nation's scholarship may be left. Thus it is that Dr. Adam Smith has, by what we cannot help regarding as an unlucky generalization, transferred his masterly argument for freedom in trade, and transferred it in all its secularity, to the question of literary and religious establishments. It is needless, by any artificial encouragement, to stimulate the supply of mercantile commodities beyond what the nation shall spontaneously require. And by many it has been held alike needless to stimulate, by artificial encouragement, the supply either of literary or christian instruction beyond what the nation shall spontaneously require. And so, opposition to endowments, whether of a scholastic or an eccle-

siastical nature, has assumed, in some degree, a philosophical aspect; or, which is still more imposing, it stands forth with a certain aspect of noble and generous liberty.

5. This hostility to the cause of such endowments meets also with powerful reinforcement from other quarters. In addition to those who have arrayed themselves against them on speculative principles, or as the disciples of a school, there are many who view them with an evil eye, from a secret disaffection towards the existing or established order of things. It would appear that, in this country, where a political opposition is often so powerful, and perhaps at all times so necessary, there is engendered, in regard to them, from this source alone, an adverse feeling, the leaven of a certain distaste or dislike for these endowments. One of the mightiest bulwarks in the hands of an administration, for perpetuating their own security and strength, is their church and university patronage—nor should we wonder, therefore, if it be one of those objects of attack against which the hostility of assailants is directed. Among our more temperate oppositionists, this feeling may amount to little more than coldness towards a system of literary and ecclesiastical benefices. But many are the fiery and resolute spirits of our age with whom it amounts to a fierce and keen antipathy. This we hold to be a reigning ingredient in the spirit of radicalism, whose

champions eye, with like disdain, the pampered sluggards of our church, and the monks of our colleges.

6. Certain it is, that, by a corrupt and careless exercise of patronage, much has been done to call forth, if not to justify, even the warmest invectives that have been uttered upon this subject. When one thinks of the high and the holy ends to which an established priesthood might be made subservient, it is quite grievous to observe the sordid politics which have to do with so many of our ecclesiastical nominations. Endowments cease to be respectable when, in the hands of a calculating statesman, they degenerate into the instruments by which he prosecutes his game of ambition; or, when employed as the bribes of political subserviency, they expose either our church or our universities to be trodden under foot by the unseemly inroads of mere office-mongers. It is thus that a land may at length be provoked to eject from its borders the establishment either of an indolent or immoral clergy, wherewith it is burdened, and to look, without regret, on the spoliation or the decay of revenue in colleges. It is truly not to be wondered at, if the poverty neither of lazy priests, nor of lazy and luxurious professors, should meet with sympathy from the public. The same generous triumph that was felt on the destruction of the old monasteries, still continues to be felt on the destruction of every old and use-

less frame-work; so that, when either a church becomes secularized,—or universities, instead of being the living fountain-heads, become the dormitories of literature, they will, sooner or later, be swept off from the country by the verdict of popular condemnation.

7. The evils of a corrupt ecclesiastical patronage are more patent to society at large; but the evils of a corrupt literary patronage are not less revolting, or less fitted to scandalize the feelings of those who are exposed, in the place which they happen to occupy, to the painful observation of them. They are evils to which, we should imagine, a provincial college may be more peculiarly liable; and especially, if it have become the freehold of some great courtier, who, awake to no generous impulse of literary enthusiasm himself, can make unfeeling havoc of that learning which is so fitted to grace and dignify a land, at the shrine of his own ignoble politics. It completes the heartless deformity of such a spectacle, when the subordinate agents of this foul desecration do themselves mingle in the proceedings of the academic body, in virtue of the place or the occupancy which they so unworthily hold within the venerable walls. It is truly a wretched contemplation, when, in the busy management of present or pending vacancies, one can behold the play of no other elements than the basest elements of sordidness. The effect is, that those chairs whence the richest wisdom and

philosophy might have emanated on the youth of our nation, are remorselessly filled by individuals who may have nought whatever of the breath, or temperament, or talent of academic men. Their literary corporation may become, in every way, as coarse and unintellectual, as any secular corporation in the land. And we are not to wonder if its respectability cannot long withstand this gothic invasion of lordly power, and reckless or unprincipled patronage.

8. In these various ways, then, the cause, whether of literary or religious endowments, has fallen into discredit; and he who undertakes to plead for them, has strong prepossessions to strive against. The tendency is, to treat learning as we should any marketable commodity; that is, leave it to the effective demand of those who may incline to purchase it, and which demand is sure to meet, as in every other instance, with a proportionate supply. In this way, it is imagined that the public eye will cease to be offended by the spectacle of an obnoxious patronage, and that we shall have the same security for a sound, and good, and valuable literature, that we have for sound and good articles in ordinary trade; that is, free choice amongst the buyers, meeting with an equal and unfettered competition amongst the sellers or providers of the thing in question. This monoply of education will cease, it is argued, when the bounty or the exclusive privilege is withdrawn from it; and the

impression, founded on an obscure analogy is, that, as by the abolition of all other monopolies, the public will be better served. We have no doubt of a preference, in many minds, for the London University over those of Oxford and Cambridge, grounded on the economic consideration which we now specify, and greatly strengthened by the experience of many corrupt appointments, and of much indolence and inefficiency in these privileged seats of learning. Nevertheless, though in opposition both to popular feeling, and to the principles of a certain philosophic school, we venture to plead the cause of literary and ecclesiastical endowments, convinced as we are that Learning, on the one hand, and Christianity on the other, would suffer from the extinction of them in the land.

9. For, first, Learning is not like an article of ordinary merchandize, or at least is not like to it in that only respect which would make endowments unnecessary. It is not true that, upon this artificial encouragement being withdrawn, there would remain an adequate encouragement in the native and spontaneous demand of the people for education. There is an utter dissimilarity between the mental appetite for knowledge, and the physical appetite for those necessaries, or even those luxuries of life, which constitute the great materials of commerce. It is not with the desire of knowledge, as it is with the desire of food. Generally

speaking, the more ignorant a man is, the more satisfied he is to remain so. But the more hungry a man is, the less satisfied he is to remain so. In the one case, the starvation of the mind is followed up by the apathy of an utter disregard for the food of the mind. In the other case, the starvation of the body is followed up by the agony of an intolerable desire after the food of the body, and to appease which any exertion or sacrifice will be made. There is no such appetite for knowledge as will secure a spontaneous and originating movement towards it, on the part of those who need to be instructed. There is such an appetite for food as will secure a spontaneous and originating movement towards it, on the part of those who need to be subsisted. In the matter of education, the supply of the article cannot be confided to the operation of demand and supply; for there is not a sufficiently effective demand. There is an abundant guarantee in the laws and constitution of sentient nature, for an effective demand in the matter of human subsistence.

10. It is this difference truly in the strength of the desire, or the demand, which forms the real distinction between the two cases; so that, while an endowment may be necessary in the one, it may, in the other, be wholly uncalled for. Government does not need to erect shops for the sale of the necessaries of life, or to help out, by a salary to the dealers, that price which customers,

rather than want the necessaries, are willing to give for them. But Government may need to erect schools, and to help out, by a salary to teachers, that price which the people are not willing to give for education. It is because of the strength of the physical appetite, and because of the languor of the intellectual or the spiritual appetite, that the same political economy which is sound in matters of trade, is not sound in matters either of literary or christian instruction. This is a subject on which the people need to be met half way. The motion for their education will not be begun, or be made, in the first instance, by themselves. It must therefore be made for them by others. A people sunk in ignorance will not emerge from it by any voluntary or self-originated act of their own. In proportion to their want of knowledge, is their want of care for it. It is as necessary to create hunger amongst them, as it is to make the provision. They will not go in quest of scholarship. The article must be offered to them ; and offered to them with such recommendations of a payment that is moderate, and a place that is patent and easily accessible, as may at least draw their notice, and call forth their demand for it.

11. And after the aggressive movement has been made in this way ; after, for example, the school-house has been raised, and a moderate school-fee has been proclaimed throughout its vicinity, there

is a charm in the very juxtaposition and name of
such an edifice, which will at length operate more
powerfully on the side of general education, than
even the argument of its cheapness. Some families will avail themselves of such an arrangement
at the outset; and others, by the mere force of
imitation, will be led to follow them; and the official fabric, known to all the neighbours by its familiar and oft-repeated designation, will at length
bind itself to the habits and affections of them all.
What was at first an occasional practice will grow
in time to a constant and regular one, till at length
the scholarship of the young shall become one of
those recognized and established decencies which
all hold to be incumbent upon them. It will come
to be incorporated with the habits of families, and
be transmitted from one generation to another
with the mechanical certainty of any local or geo-
graphical peculiarity in the customs of the people.
They never would have made the initial movement
themselves, either for building the school, or for
making out a full remuneration to the schoolmaster. Yet, when once the school is built for them,
and partial payment has been made of the fee, by
means of a salary, the fabric thus raised and endowed becomes a signal of invitation, that is at
length responded to by all the families of the district. So that, while, without this expedient, the
country may, in respect of scholarship, be one de-
solate and unprovided waste, or at least present

many large and intervening tracts, among the rare occasional spaces reclaimed by a gratuitous philanthropy; with this expedient, the blessings of popular education may come to be fully and equally diffused over the surface of the land.

12. Hence the universality of education in the lowland parishes of Scotland. The people are not taught gratuitously; for, by a small quarterly payment, they are made to share in the expense of the education of their families; but the remaining share is, by the law, devolved upon others. It consists of a salary which enables the schoolmaster to teach upon moderate terms, and of a school and school-house, with a garden, by which education is visibly obtruded upon the notice of every little vicinity. To this extent, the offer of education may be said to have been made; and it is an offer that has been met by the nearly unexcepted consent and co-operation of the Scottish peasantry. Had it not been for this aggression upon them from without, the people would have felt no impulse towards education from within, and so would have stood fast in their primeval ignorance. It is the scholastic establishment of our land that has called its people out of that quiescence and lethargy in which every people are, by nature, so firmly imbedded. It has drawn them forth of the stronghold; and awoke from their dull imprisonment, those higher and greater faculties which lie so profoundly asleep among a people, who, till ad-

dressed by some such influence, are wholly engrossed with animal wants and animal enjoyments. In other words, it is to a great national endowment that our national character is beholden. Those generous sensibilities, which have been so vehemently wreaked in ire and hostility against the cause, may perhaps be pacified, and even enlisted upon its side, when it comes to be understood that it is to an endowment in fact, to that against which some of the sons of liberty and patriotism have been heard to lift their eloquence, that Scotland stands indebted for her well-taught and well-conditioned peasantry.*

13. But more than this. We now see that the parochial establishment of schools not only provided, in part, the learning, but, what was of greater importance still, created the appetite for it in the minds of the people. Nor is this an appetite that would go suddenly into extinction, even were the establishment swept away. After the habit of scholarship has been formed and matured among a people, it might, though left to its own energy, abide and linger with them for several generations. There was, in the first instance, no native demand for the article to encourage a supply of it; but, in the course of time, such a taste, and such a demand may have been excited, that the people, now led to regard education almost in

---

* See Note B. Appendix.

the light of a necessary, may, on the aid of endowments being withdrawn, be willing to part with the whole price for it rather than want it altogether. In proof of this, we may refer to those cases where the people are dissatisfied with the established schoolmaster, either from his incapacity or from some other cause. They send their children to a subscription school; and, in the shape of a higher fee than the parochial one, give the whole price for education. The same thing is observed in towns or populous parishes, where the number of families outstrips the established means of instruction. The people now do what they would not have done a few generations ago. Independently of the establishment, and without any aid from its provisions, but on the strength of their own payments alone, they defray the whole expense of their children's scholarship. But it is in virtue of a taste which the establishment has created. Its endowments have thus elevated our plebeian classes, and given them this higher mental ambition. But for those endowments, the people of the land would still have been in a state of mental apathy; and, to the parochial establishment of schools, do we owe not merely a provision of knowledge for our peasantry, but the creation among them of an appetite for knowledge beyond what itself can at all times supply.

14. It were a mistake, however, to imagine, that, after having achieved this service, it would

be safe to dispense with an establishment, or that, after having raised the appetite for education, the future supply of education might be left to the working of this appetite alone. This, at best, were a hazardous experiment; and, even though it could be attempted without any decline on the part of the common people from the level of their present scholarship, the upholding of an establishment were still desirable as an instrument for raising, and that indefinitely, the standard of popular education.

15. It is thus that the effect which we now advert to may be made palpable. Conceive, that, with the aid of the parochial endowment, the average quarterly payment for education is at present two shillings and sixpence; but that the people, rather than forego an advantage which they have now learned to value, would, of their own accord, pay five shillings a quarter. It would, in this case, be all the more safe to pull down the establishment, and leave the interest of education to be sustained by the now effective demand of the people for it. But a far better use to make of their now advanced taste would be, by retaining the establishment, to advance the quality of that scholarship which it was wont to deal out among the families. If, for two shillings and sixpence a quarter, with the endowment superadded, men can be found to furnish the people with their present homelier education; then, for five shillings a quar-

ter, with the same endowment, men could be found to furnish them with a higher education. This effect might be enhanced by a contemporaneous increase of the salary along with the fees; and those schools where English reading, and writing, and the most elementary arithmetic, are now all that is taught, might come to have a higher and more extended course, including a classical education for some, and a popular mathematics, with its most useful application for others, and even natural history, in some of its more pleasing and accessible departments, for all. Such seems to be the readiest way of bringing teachers, more accomplished than before, into contact with the general population; while they, on the other hand, may be carried indefinitely upwards, as if, by successive lifts from one generation to another, along the career of an ascending scholarship. The cause of popular education would thus move forward with other things. And these endowed schools, at every step in this advancement of the plebeian taste, might, by a concurrent force, help the people forward to those higher acquisitions after which they had now learned to aspire."*

---

* To every one acquainted with the Parish Schools of Scotland during the last thirty years, the improvement which has taken place in popular education must be quite obvious. It were most desirable, however, that the salaries of the masters were augmented, even though, to maintain the balance between that part of their income which is fixed, and that part of it which fluctuates with their own exertions, there should along with this be a con-

16. But this virtue which there is in endowments for giving effect, in future, to the eventual demand of the people for a higher scholarship, carries the attention upward to those higher seminaries which exist at present, for the education of the more affluent classes in society. It is a mistaken imagination, that their affluence alone forms a sufficient guarantee for such an effectual demand as could itself call forth all the philosophy and all the science that have flourished in time past, and that might be made to flourish still more under a system of endowments. There might be enough of individuals in society, who have the means of giving an adequate price for this higher scholarship. But there might not be enough of individuals who have the taste that would incline them to the expensive purchase of such a scholarship. What is true of a people in total ignorance in reference to elementary learning, is also true of the people who have been only schooled thus far in reference to the more arduous and loftier acquisitions of learning. They who occupy the lowest platform, even that of entire destitution in regard to knowledge, will

---

temporaneous increase of the fees. In this way, the burden of the whole augmentation would be divided between the heritors and the parents of the scholars. There is a very general disposition to under-rate the capabilities of the latter, and, accordingly, it is alleged that they are not able to bear their share of the burden. They, notwithstanding, do pay larger fees than they did half a century ago—and they are often found, for the sake of a better education to their children, to pay the much larger fees of a subscription school.

not, if left to themselves, aspire and move upward
to the platform which is immediately above them.
But neither will they who occupy this second ascent, look, with a sufficient force of desirousness,
above their existing level, so as to work themselves
up to the third or fourth stages of this ascending
progression. If, at the outset, there was such an
apathy to knowledge in the land, that endowments
were called for to originate and continue even the
humblest kind of scholarship; still there is such a
want of all lofty mental ambition, that endowments
are yet called for to originate and sustain the
higher kinds of scholarship. When people are at
zero in the scale of knowledge, it is not by any
native buoyancy of theirs, but by the application
of a force from without, that they are elevated one
degree in the scale. And, when raised thus far,
it is still not by any inherent buoyancy, but by an
external power, that they are brought and upheld
higher in the scale. Now, they are the universities, the endowed and privileged universities, which
act with this external power upon society. They
are so many forces whose tendency is to draw the
people upward from that state, as to education, to
which they would subside, and in which they
would settle, if left to themselves. Insomuch
that, upon the existence of such endowments, well
patronized, turns all the difference between a high
and a low state of philosophy in a nation.

17. To make this familiar by instances. A

people, though universally accomplished by schools
in elementary learning, will not lift up themselves
by any inherent buoyancy of their own, to the
level of that learning which should be taught in
colleges. Over the whole country, there is not
enough of spontaneous demand for the higher mathematics, to guarantee a sufficient maintenance
for even so much as one teacher. There is an
effective demand, we are aware, for as much of
the science as is popular and practical, and of
which the uses are quite palpable and immediate.
A man without the aid of endowments will gain a
livelihood, by teaching any thing that is of obvious
application either to an art or a calling which is
gainful. But, for all that is arduous and sublime
in mathematics, for the methods of that higher
calculus, the uses of which lie far remote, or are
wholly invisible to the general understanding, for
those lofty devices and inventions of analysis, by
which we may hope to accomplish solutions hitherto
impracticable, or to unravel mysteries in nature,
which have yet eluded the keenest search of philosophy,—for all these, we contend, there is no
such public request as might foster the growth
and the production of them to the extent that is at
all desirable. The science which germinates these
in sufficient abundance, can only flourish under
the shade of endowments. Without this artificial
encouragement, the philosophy of our land would
wax feeble, and dwindle at length into evanes-

cence; and in all the prouder and nobler walks of discovery, we must consent to be outrun in glory by other nations.

18. Here it occurs to us to say, that what Dr. Smith has stigmatised as a statute of apprenticeship in colleges, is of still greater effect in the encouragement of all loftier sciences, than what is properly an endowment. The salary enables a teacher of these sciences to live, and admit scholars on a moderate fee to his source of instruction. In this way the obstacle of expense is lessened. But it is not by the removal of an obstruction alone that a sufficient number of pupils will be drawn to a class of arduous and recondite philosophy. There must, beside this, be the operation of an attractive force; and we fear, that, for the purpose of giving sufficient intensity to such a force, something must be superadded to that native charm which is conceived to lie in the scholarship itself. And it is thus that the vulgar incentive of gain has been made to reinforce those higher incentives, which operate only on a few of the more ethereal spirits of our race. This is done by a statute of apprenticeship. To make use of a Scottish term in an argument, the purpose of which is to expound the system of Scottish universities, it is done by *thirling* to certain of our classes all those students who are under process of education for some one of the learned professions, and making a complete course of attendance upon these classes an indis-

pensable qualification for the holding of its lucrative offices. For example, no one can receive a license, or, of course, be admitted to a living in the church, who has not fulfilled a university course of natural philosophy. And we have no doubt that, to this regulation, the college classes throughout Scotland of this noble science, are indebted for at least a sevenfold greater attendance than they would otherwise enjoy.

19. It is not a pure mental ambition which carries to these classes the majority of their pupils. Yet we have no doubt that during the attendance there, such an ambition is in very many instances awakened. The love of science was not the impellent force at the outset, which urged forward such a number of disciples to its lessons. But after they had been thus brought within the view of science, it recommended its own loveliness to the taste of many an aspiring intellect, that would have otherwise been lost to the cause of learning. Philosophy did not attract them by any native charm of her own, till, by the power of a grosser inducement, they were brought within the sphere of attraction. But it is a prodigious service to philosophy thus to bring them within the sphere; and this service is done by our statutes of apprenticeship. There have been thousands in our land, the enamoured votaries of science, who never would have felt the generous inspiration, had it not been evoked by the eloquence and the demon-

strations of an academic chair, attended by them not of free will, but in conformity to those qualifying statutes, which have been so much complained of. The latent spark that was in them would still have remained in its dormancy, had it not been for the kindred touch which developed it. Philosophy at length became the mistress of their affections, but not till they were made to see her engaging mien, and to hear the music of her voice. It was a good thing to have conducted them, even though as if by a hand of violence, along the way of her fascinations. It is well that the youth of our country should thus be brought in yearly hundreds within reach of the academic influence. It will not tell beneficially upon all; but it will elicit a responsive sympathy from those who have the kindred spirit and enthusiasm within them. The flame is not awakened by the property of spontaneous ignition; but it brightens into life and lustre, at a shrine of costly maintenance, and of hallowed guardianship.

20. There are five college classes of natural philosophy in Scotland; and, by a statute of apprenticeship in our church, every aspirant to the ministry must pass through one or other of these, ere he can be admitted to his theological studies. We feel quite confident in affirming, that, but for this statute, with salaries to professorships, there would not be enough of attendance from the whole land, for securing a decent livelihood even to one pro-

fessor of the science. And this scarcity of pupils would be aggravated, just in proportion to the pure, and lofty, and philosophic character of the course. If, for example, it were the transcendental aim of the professor to accomplish his students for the perusal of La Place's Mechanique Celeste, we doubt if all Scotland together would furnish him with so many as twelve, that would listen to his demonstrations. At this rate, it is obvious, that no class could be formed, just because the proceeds of it could afford no adequate maintenance to a teacher. This arduous and recondite philosophy behoved to disappear, simply by ceasing to be transmitted from one generation to annother. The record of it, in unknown hieroglyphics, might still be found in our libraries; but it would have no place in the living intellect of our nation.

21. Still there would be a natural philosophy taught, and even, it is possible, numerously attended by those who, in obedience to their own taste, repaired in crowds to the exhibition of its wonders. But to attract these crowds, there behoved to be a woful descent from the dignity of a high academic model. All repulsive mathematics would be exploded; and, instead of being conducted through the mysteries of astronomical science, by that arduous path on which Newton trod with gigantic footstep, it would be held enough by the pigmies of a superficial age, that they

learned of orbs and of cycles from the evolutions of an orrery. The profounder studies of nature would be abandoned; and for these we should behold experimental class-rooms, filled, it might be, with hundreds who came to bestow their silly admiration on the puerilities and the paradoxes of a wretched necromancy. To uphold the severe intellectual training of our land, there must be endowments for the teacher, and compulsory statutes of apprenticeship for the taught. Without these, the philosophy of our land would sink down from the colossal strength and stateliness of a former generation, into a mere popular empiricism. It would lose the masculine vigour which it once had in the Augustan age of England's mathematics, and fast drivel into effeminacy, with nought to feed upon but the syllabub lectures of fashionable institutes.*

22. When a distinguished Professor of this country hazarded the assertion, that there were not twelve British mathematicians who could read La Place's great work with any tolerable facility, we fear that, alive as the whole nation is to its honour in the field of war, or political rivalship, there are

---

* It is well, however, that these seminaries of slighter education, whether under the name of institutes for the wealthier, or of mechanic schools for the working classes, should be multiplied to the uttermost. They bring up the pupils who attend them to a higher grade of scholarship—but it remains as desirable as ever, and indeed more so, that the scholarship of universities should be of the highest possible character, should be at the summit of the scale.

but few indeed of the nation who felt the affront
of being left so immeasurably behind in this highest
of all intellectual rivalship, both by France and
Prussia. It is verily one of the worst symptoms
of our degeneracy, that almost nowhere, in the
most cultured society, is the expression of regret
ever heard, because that glory which a Newton
shed over our country has now departed from us.
Yet is it refreshing to observe in what quarter of
the island it was where the quickest sensibility was
felt for the honour of British mathematics. It was
in the academic bowers,—the lettered retreats of
Cambridge. *There* the somewhat precipitate
charge of our northern collegian met with a re-
sentment in which so few can sympathize; and
there also, we rejoice to believe, that it met its best
refutation. And if, in that wealthy seat of learning, even twenty individuals could be found to
master the difficulties of the French analysis, this,
in the midst of surrounding degradation and
poverty, of itself speaks volumes for endowments.

23. There would need to be a similar descent,
too, from the altitudes of moral and metaphysical
science, ere a professor, who depended wholly on
the spontaneous demand of his pupils, could as-
semble a sufficient number of them to enable him
to earn for himself a livelihood. We venture to
affirm, that, but for a statute of apprenticeship,
Dr. Thomas Brown could not have upheld a class
of fifty students, even in the metropolis of Scotland,

and that to enlarge its numbers, he behoved to have let himself down from those arduous heights of recondite and original speculation on which he acquired such eminent distinction in the walk of mental philosophy. In other words, the lustre and the glory of his discoveries might have been altogether lost to our land, had it not been for that system of endowments which we advocate, though sometimes stigmatized as an odious and illiberal monopoly. It is just such a monopoly as secures to the nation a better article than the nation, by any free and popular movement, would have sought for itself. For philosophy, to be made palatable, must be diluted, and made of easy digestion. Like other wholesome draughts, it cannot be entirely left to the choice of those who are bettered by the administration of it. A certain degree of compulsion is necessary; and it is just such a compulsion as a statute of apprenticeship secures, and by which it commands a numerous attendance on classes that would otherwise revolt by the depth and difficulty of their subjects. There is another way, indeed, by which to overcome this native distaste of the popular understanding for the profound, the solid, and the elaborate. There might be presented to it declamation instead of disquisition; the effusions of a shining but superficial eloquence, instead of the processes or the results of a powerful analysis; an offering of sweets and flowers to the imagination, instead of a call upon the intellect to gird itself for combat with the sophistries of Hume, or for accompanying the sounder argumentations of Bacon, and Locke, and Clarke, and Reid, and Campbell, and Butler. In this way, a class-room might be thronged with auditors, lured by the oratory of him whose lectureship is bespangled all over with the tinsel of a gaudy sentimentalism. But it is evident, that such a wretched compromise as this with the appetite of the multitude, is not the way by which to uphold a firm staple of philosophy in our land. What we gain in popular fascination, we shall lose in weight, and in massiveness; and, with no demand for the products of arduous or severe thought, we shall sink down into a generation of little minds and of little men.

24. It is certainly desirable, that a Professor should be placed above the reach of a temptation so humiliating, as that of stepping down from a higher to a lower walk in science, for the purpose of there meeting with a proper number of students. Rather, if necessary, let a greater number of stepping-stones be provided, by which they may be helped upward to his level, than that he should let down his efforts, and waste himself on such lessons as are merély popular and elementary. In other words, let the system of education in schools be extended, and a far higher scholarship exacted from all who propose to enter within the limits of a college. There should be as great a distinction between the work of a university and that of a

school, as there is between manhood and boyhood.
Even the language professors, relieved in a greater
measure than they now are from the drudgery of
those lessons, of which the sole object is to increase
the practical acquaintance of their pupils with
Greek and Latin, should be able to expatiate more
at large on the field of taste, and criticism, and
ancient history. In this event, we should not have
such juvenile classes as we have at present; for the
change of practice would give rise to a later, and,
therefore, also to a more limited attendance of
students. It would operate against the pecuniary
interest of the professor, in deducting from the
number of university scholars; but it would operate
also in dignifying his employment by the additional
vigour and manhood that might then be imparted
to university scholarship.

25. The work of a teacher may be regarded as
twofold. It is his busines, *first*, To conduct what
may be called the gymnastics of education; and,
secondly, By his own proper and peculiar arrange-
ments, or by his own original views, to illustrate
and extend its topics. In the former employment,
it is his object to convey to the students' minds
the existent lessons of science or scholarship, whether these lessons have been bequeathed to him by
others, or have been matured by himself. In the
latter employment, he acts the higher, though not
the more useful, part of either, by his powers of
discovery making new lessons, or by his powers of

distribution making a new assortment of them.
By the one exercise, he may guide his pupils over
all the actual philosophy or literature of his department: by the other, he may shed upon it a
brighter illumination, or push forward its boundaries. It is obvious, that, in the classical and
mathematical provinces of education, there is
greater room for the first of these offices, while in
mental or moral, or economical science, there is
greater room for the second. It would be well if,
previous to their admission into Universities, our
youth described a more extended course of task-
work and examination among the details of practical scholarship; not, indeed, so as altogether to
supersede taskwork and examination after they
had left the more juvenile seminaries, but so that
they might be better prepared, both by their habits
and their years, for accompanying the professors
in their most original speculations, and through
the most arduous of their enterprises. It is thus
that the country would secure a constant supply
of those more exalted functionaries in science, part
of whose vocation it is to build her up to a prouder
altitude than before, or to extend the range of her
discoveries. They might become the chief instruments for the advancement of philosophy,—the
labourers who, by successive lifts, from age to age,
made perpetual additions to the intellectual and
literary wealth of our species.

26. A university should not be a mere gymna-

sium. We admit that it is too little so in Scotland, and perhaps too much so in England. Certain it is, however, we repeat, that it were most desirable, if in our own country, the preparations of the gymnasium were greatly further advanced at the entrance of our young men into colleges. This could be managed by the establishment of a thorough scholastic system in each of our university towns. If our students came to us more advanced both in years and in scholarship, then the original and excursive and independent methods of our professors in all the higher sciences would not be so indefensible;—when, instead of having to address an audience of boys, they felt themselves sustained, even in their loftiest endeavours, by the intelligent sympathy of those who had now reached the man-hood of their understandings. It is obvious, that, in this way, the style of education might be indefinitely heightened; while, as the fruit of the services of those who laboured in the upper departments of it, there might come forth of our universities, from time to time, the richest contributions to our literature and philosophy. A college might thus be an organ, not merely for bringing the scholarship of a country up to the level of its science, but for creating a higher science, wherewith still more to raise and refine its scholarship.

27. The colleges of Scotland, with all the defects which attach to them as practical seminaries, have, in regard to the latter of these two functions, been

of the most important service in promoting both
the honour and the advancement of our national
literature. The truth is, that greatly more than
half the distinguished authorship of our land is
professorial; and, till the present generation, we
scarcely remember, with the exception of Hume
in philosophy, and Thomson in poetry, any of our
eminent writers who did not achieve, or at least
germinate, all their greatest works while labouring
in their vocation of public instructors in one or
other of our universities.* Nay, generally speaking, these publications were the actual product of
their labour in the capacity of teachers ; and passed
into authorship through the medium of their respective chairs. Whatever charges may have been
preferred against the methods of university education in Scotland, it is at least fortunate for the
literary character of our nation, that the professors
have not felt, in conducting the business of their
appointments, as if they were dealing altogether
with boys. To this we owe, the manly, and original, and independent treatment, which so many of
them have bestowed on their appropriate sciences,
and by which they have been enabled to superadd
one service to another. They have not only taught
philosophy; they have also both rectified its doc-

* But we should not forget the names of Monboddo, and Hailes, and
Kaimes, and Gillies, and Macknight, and Robert Walker, and Henry
M'Kenzie, who, though still alive, ranks more properly with the distinguished
men of a former age.

trines, and added their own views and discoveries to the mass of pre-existent learning. They, in fact, have been the chief agents in enlarging our country's science; and it is mainly, though not exclusively, to them that Scotland is indebted for her eminence and high estimation in the republic of letters. For the truth of this averment in regard to natural science, we may appeal to the works of Colin Maclaurin, and Robert Simson, and Matthew Stewart, and Wilson of Glasgow, and Dr. Black, and Professor Robison, and the Monros, and Gregories, and Cullen, of Edinburgh, and Hamilton of Aberdeen, and Playfair and Leslie; and, in regard to moral and political science, we appeal to the writings of Hutcheson, and Adam Smith, and Reid, and Miller, and Campbell, and Beattie, and Dugald Stewart, and Tytler, and Ferguson, and Brown. We would, further, appropriate to the honour of our Universities, the publications of Principal Robertson in history, and Dr. Hill in theology, and Blair and Barron in taste and criticism, and Dr. John Hunter of St. Andrew's in classical learning, and the philosophy of grammar.* With one or two exceptions, all the authorship which we have now enumerated was of direct college fabrication; in the first instance, designed

* Dr. John Hill, and Professor Dalzell of Edinburgh; Professors Jardine and Young of Glasgow, though the last unfortunately has bequeathed little to posterity in the way of authorship, are worthy of a high place in the enumeration of Scottish Professors.

and executed for the class-room, till fitted, by successive rectifications, for presentation on a wider theatre. The colleges were the manufactories of all this literature, which they never could have been, had professors been mere practical teachers; and hence, if, along with the expedients for giving that more practical character to the education of Scotland, which it certainly requires, something be not done to uphold the independence and the contemplative leisure of its professors, the nation may come to be shorn of its intellectual greatness.

28. Dr. Smith, who appears, in his Wealth of Nations, to have erred so egregiously in his economic views on the subject of literary and ecclesiastical endowments, gives, in the same work, some very sound and admirable observations, the results, we have no doubt, of his own professorial experience, on the effect of professorial work, in perfecting the views of a master, and enabling him at length to come forth with a mature and well digested course of lessons on his own peculiar subject, for the instruction of the public at large. It is thus that his own Theory of Moral Sentiments was ripened for publication; and it is thus that his still more enduring Theory of National Wealth was at least germinated, if not a great way advanced, at the time when he relinquished his academic situation. We cannot, indeed, imagine a more favourable condition for the formation of a great literary work that shall have solid and en-

during excellence, than that which is occupied by an ardent and devoted professor, whose course, by means of reiterated elaborations, receives a slow, it may be, but withal a sure and progressive improvement. Only conceive him to be fully possessed with his subject, and giving the full strength of his mind to its elucidation; and then, with the advantages of perseverance, and time, and frequent periodical, reiteration of the topics of his lectureship, he is assuredly in the best possible circumstances for bequeathing to posterity some lasting memorial of industry or genius. It is by the remodellings and the revisals, every year, of his yet imperfect preparations; it is by strengthening what is weak, and further illustrating what is obscure, and fortifying some position or principle by a new argument, and aiding the conception of his disciples by some new image or new analogy; it is thus that the product of his official labours may annually acquire increasing excellence, and gradually approximate to a state of faultlessness, till at length it comes forth in a work of finished execution, and becomes a permanent addition to the classic and literary wealth of the nation. It is not so often by flashes of inspiration, as by power and patience united, that works are reared and ripened for immortality. It is not in the hasty effervescence of a mind under sudden and sanguine excitement, that a service so precious to society is generally rendered. It is when a strong, and, at the same

time, a steadfast mind gives its collected energies
to the task ; and not only brings its own independent judgment, but laboriously collecting the lights
of past erudition, brings them also to bear on the
subject of its investigations ; it is thus that treatises
are written, and systems are framed, which eclipse
the volumes of their predecessor, and, taking their
place, become themselves the luminaries of future
ages.

29. Such objects as these never can be carried
into effect without endowments. The leisure and
independence of the men who wield these high
services, must in some way or other be secured.
This, indeed, is as good as conceded by Dr. Smith
himself, in the beautiful exposition which he gives
of the comparative states of literature in England
and Scotland.* In the former country, the church
is better endowed than the universities, which,
therefore, generally becomes the ultimate landing
place of her more eminent literary men, the line
of preferment being in that direction. In the latter
country, the universities were, in the days of Smith
at least, better endowed than the church, which
reversed the line of preferment, so that, in as far
as patronage was associated with merit, the men
of abilities who signalized themselves in Scotland,
found their final destination to be among the em-
ployments of a college. In other words, there is

* See Note C, Appendix.

a process for the absorption of talent going on
in England—the occupier of an ecclesiastical office
there, in so far as he is removed from the stimulus
and the sympathies of academic converse, not being in such likely circumstances for literary exertion. A process, the opposite of this, is going on
in Scotland—where the conspicuous talent of the
church is more drawn to its universities, and so, in
the midst of a congenial element, and amongst congenial duties, expands into greater power and pro-
ductiveness, than in any other situation. It is
thus that while more than half the literature of Scotland is professorial, it is a much smaller fraction,
indeed, of the literature of England which is contributed by those who are connected, by office or
by employment, with either of its universities.

30. Now, from this fact, the inference deducible
in favour of endowments is obvious. They contain in them that adhesive virtue, which both
draws men of literary power to the places of
literary employment, and detains them there.
Were the value of our endowments lessened, the
process of Scotland might be reversed into that of
England. Or, were the endowments done away,
and the remuneration of lofty science left to the
payments of those who had a spontaneous demand
for it, then all lofty science would depart from
our universities; and the men who were most
capable of sustaining the toils and advancing the
honours of an arduous philosophy, would easily

find a more liberal reward for the exercise of their talents, in some of the gainful walks of civil or secular employment. We have sometimes regretted, that it was in the power even of one of our most affluent noblemen, to tempt Dr. Smith away from his professorship in Glasgow; or, if the injury which literature suffered, in consequence of this divorce, was more than compensated by the gain that accrued to economic science, from his opportunities of travel and observation on the continent, there is at least one, and that the last of his preferments, which must ever be deplored by the friends of philosophy. We allude to his appointment as a commissioner of customs, which blasted one of his greatest literary undertakings. The public lost by this, his projected work on jurisprudence; and all they got in return was a service which hundreds could have rendered as well as he, among the details and drudgeries of an official employment. We hold it to have been quite a gothic deed in our country, thus to fritter away the fine mental energies of one of the most accomplished of her sons, by setting him down with mere penmen or practitioners at a board. Surely it would have been better, if a provision as ample as this incongruous situation afforded, could have been found for such a man within the asylum of a college, where, exempted from the fatigues and the vulgarities of ordinary business, and in the midst of a kindred society, he might

have been upheld at a high pitch of literary effort
and enthusiasm to the last.* He ought to have
been sustained, to the end of his days, in the simple
and venerable capacity of a sage; and that was a
disgraceful economy, which rifled from him his
intellectual leisure, and robbed the commonwealth
of all those fruits, wherewith, in the mellowness
and maturity of his wisdom, he might still further
have enriched the authorship of his land.

31. Yet hostility to such endowments often
assumes the garb of a generous and high-minded
patriotism. This is an evil fruit, or rather one of
the evil accompaniments, of our liberty. Its jealousy, both of expense and of patronage, has given
rise to a penurious system of encouragement for
literary merit; and in the style of its rewards,
when it does bestow them, we behold at times all
the grossness of the mercantile spirit. It is because there is so much of the *a la bourgeoise* in
the reigning policy of the land, that it gives no
offence to the feelings even of our most refined
and polished society, when told of Sir Isaac Newton having been master and worker of the Mint,

---

* We should feel no difficulty in assigning to the Principal of a College
duties of such magnitude and importance, as might well be pleaded both
for the prolongation of the office in each university, and for the ample
endowment of it. But, even though it should still retain that character of
a sinecure into which it has now lapsed for nearly half a century, we
would still regret either the abolition of the office or the abridgment of its
emoluments. It should form the natural reward of men distinguished by
their literary services, and whose names might throw a splendour on the
societies over which they preside. Scotland is far too scantily provided in
such situations.

and Dr. Smith commissioner of customs, and Henry
Mackenzie being comptroller of the Tax-Office,
and Wordsworth an agent for stamps in the county
of Westmoreland, and Dugald Stewart, recorder
of prices in the Edinburgh Gazette, and, lastly,
Sir Walter Scott a clerk to the Court of Session.
It is the dread of that popular odium which attaches
to pensions and sinecures, that gives rise to such
incongruous and untasteful combinations, and
which, under the mask of purity and public virtue, has impressed a certain taint of sordidness
and plebeian coarseness on this department of the
country's affairs. At the same time, the real
freedom and substantial prosperity of the inferior
classes, are in no way promoted by it; and, in
truth, it were a better tempered society, and
would be conducive to the welfare of all its classes,
if, by means of more amply rewarded talent, an
aristocracy of letters could be upholden, by which
to qualify and to soften the vulgar aristocracy of
mere rank and power.

32. We have a continued historical illustration
in favour of endowments, in the princely establishments of England. Grant that neither of her
universities has been so productive of learning as
it might have been, yet, who can imagine for a
moment, that, apart from benefactions, and under
the fostering influences of the public demand and
patronage alone, either the erudite and classic
lore of the one illustrious seminary, or the profound

science of the other, could ever have been realised.
It is, indeed, highly instructive to mark the progress of these two great literary institutes. One
cannot do so without being convinced, that, but
for the liberalities of patriotism or piety, the education of the land never would have risen to its
present altitude,—that, in no one instance, has
their constantly growing scholarship been indebted,
for any new addition, to the encouragement of an
anterior demand, or market, for science, from
without; but that it has originated in the emanating
force of some additional endowment from within, *
—that the learning which now wells out upon the
nation from these venerable fountain-heads, did
not arise at first in the shape of a previously required service by the country, and for which the
country was willing to pay; but that it arose in
the shape of a gift, which had to be pressed for
acceptance on the country, and which had to be
urged perseveringly, and against the opposition of
many moral and many natural difficulties, ere the

---

* The most recent example of this which we at present recollect, is the
endowment of a class for Political Economy in Oxford. They might have
waited for ever for a permanent establishment of this sort, had they waited
till there was a sufficient extrinsic and effective demand for the lessons of
the science, to ensure its being supported by fees alone. But now that
these lessons are obtruded on the notice of the young men attending that
University, who does not see that, on the appointment of an able lecturer,
there is the certainty of a large amount of education in this important
branch of knowledge? We should rejoice to see distinct lectureships on
Political Economy instituted and provided for in each of the Scottish
Universities.

country would be prevailed on to accept it. It is, in truth, the history of a perpetual struggle on the part of a few lofty and large-hearted men, * with the mental apathy and indolence which naturally, and, but for appliances from without, lord it over the great bulk of our species. It is only through the force of aggressive movements, and by dint of successive advances, that the cause of learning has gained, on an otherwise passive or reluctant public; or that they have laboriously and at length been nurtured into their present habits of education. Teachers had not only to be paid by endowments for their lessons; but students had to be paid, or bribed, for their attendance. There was a real practical necessity for all this forcing and fostering. The fellowships and bursaries, or scholarships, of the English colleges, have not been thrown away. They have, upon the whole, fulfilled their destination,—and to them we owe a loftier science, a far more lettered and refined society, than ever would have spontaneously arisen out of the barbarism of past generations.

33. We cannot conclude this passing notice of the Universities of England, without the mention of how much they are ennobled by those great master-spirits, those men of might and of high achievement,—the Newtons, and the Miltons, and the Drydens, and the Barrows, and the Addisons,

* See Note D, Appendix.

and the Butlers, and the Clarkes, and the Stilling-
fleets, and the Ushers, and the Foxes, and the
Pitts, and Johnsons, who, within their attic retreats,
received that first awakening, which afterwards
expanded into the aspirations and the triumphs of
loftiest genius. This is the true heraldry of colleges. Their family honour is built on the prowess
of sons, not on the greatness of ancestors; and we
will venture to say, that there are no seminaries
in Europe on which there sits a greater weight of
accumulated glory, than that which has been re-
flected, both on Oxford and Cambridge, by that
long and bright train of descendants who have
sprung from them. It is impossible to make even
the bare perusal of their names* without the feeling, that there has been summoned before the eye
of the mind, the panorama of all that has upheld
the lustre, whether of England's philosophy, or of
England's patriotism, for centuries together. We
have often thought what a meagre and stinted
literature we should have had without them; and
what, but for the two universities, would have
been the present state of science or theology in
England. These rich seminaries have been the
direct and the powerful organs for the elaboration
of both; and both would rapidly decline, as if
languishing under the want of their needful aliment,
were the endowments of colleges swept away. It

---

* See Note E, Appendix.

were a truly gothic spoliation; and the Rule of that political economy, which could seize upon their revenues, would be, in effect, as hostile to the cause of sound and elevated learning in Britain, as would be the Rule of that popular violence which could make havoc of their architecture, and savagely exult over the ruin of their libraries and halls.

34. There is much to be learned upon this subject from the failure of many sectarian academies in England.* The dissenters of that kingdom have made the richest contributions to the cause of vital Christianity, by the publication of an immensity of practical works, replete both with piety and experimental wisdom. We are not, indeed, acquainted with any department of authorship, where so much of this precious treasure is to be found as in the writings of the nonconformists. Yet it is not to be disguised, that, with all their powerful appeals to conscience, there is not among them that full and firm staple of erudition which is to be found among the divines of the Establishment, to whom, after all, the theological literature of our land is chiefly beholden.† To them we are, in the

---

* We trust that the strenuous exertions which have recently been made in favour of the Homerton and Highbury Colleges, will lead to the secure and permanent establishment of these excellent institutions. This, however, will require, I should imagine, a perseverance of liberality from year to year, on the part of contributors, whose annual subscriptions perform in fact the part of an endowment.

† But we must not here forget the lasting obligations which Lardner has conferred on the world, by those erudite and laborious researches which

main, indebted for a species of literature, which in no country of Europe is carried to such a height as among ourselves. We allude to the part which they have sustained in the deistical controversy, and to the masterly treatises wherein they have so thoroughly scrutinized and set forth the Christian argument. But it is not in the war with infidelity alone that they have signalized themselves. A bare recital of the names associated with Oxford and Cambridge would further convince us, that, from these mighty strongholds have issued our most redoubted champions of orthodoxy; and that the church of which they are the feeders and the fountain-heads, has, of all others, stood the fore-most, and wielded the mightiest polemic arm in the battles of the faith.

35. Upon the whole, then, the great argument for literary endowments is founded on the want, or the weakness of the natural appetency for literature in our species. There is not that spontaneous demand for it, which would be effective to the bringing forth of an adequate supply; and the higher the literature is, the more is it placed above the reach of any such effective demand. This is not a subject on which we can with safety wait for mankind,—but a subject on which mankind need

---

have been of so much benefit to the Christian argument. It must, at the same time, be remarked, that the most conspicuous of the early Noncon-formists belonged originally to the Church, and had the benefit of University Education.

to be assailed with offers, or which they must be
beckoned to approach by all the signals and facilities of invitation. The importunity is not, as in
many other things, on the side of the customers
who receive, but the importunity must be on the
side of the sellers or the providers, who bestow.
Rather than want the articles of ordinary merchandise, men will give a price for them above their
prime cost, so as to afford a profit. But science is
not one of these articles, and will infallibly languish and be neglected, unless it is pressed on the
acceptance of men at a price greatly below prime
cost, and the purpose of endowments is to make
up the difference. The operation of these is exemplified in miniature, when a munificent patron
of literature or the arts aids the publication of
those massy and expensive folios, for which the
demand is so limited, that all the money given by
purchasers would amount to but a fraction of the
cost. It is to his largess that the world is indebted
for all the delight or instruction which this publication affords. So is it, likewise, with the expense
of an educational apparatus; and, more especially,
when the education is of a lofty scientific character. The scholars do not yield the full remuneration; and, but for the benefactor, there would
have been no such scholarship.

36. It is mainly by the same argument that we
would vindicate the policy of ecclesiastical endowments. The necessity for the one is founded on

the natural want or weakness of the literary appetite; and the necessity for the other is founded on the natural want or weakness of the spiritual appetite. But we are sensible that each requires its own peculiar modifications, and these we shall separately discuss in the two following chapters. We shall attempt, first, a more special application of the argument to the Endowment of Colleges; and, afterwards, an application of the same general argument to the Endowment of Churches.

CHAPTER II.

MORE SPECIAL APPLICATION OF THE ARGUMENT TO COLLEGES.

1. In the days of our forefathers, the difficulty, both in Scotland and England, was to obtain a sufficient number of persons qualified for undertaking the duties of the pastoral charge. The number of vacant parishes greatly exceeded the number of competent and well educated labourers who might fill them. This scarcity, in fact, was one great impellent cause of the multiplication of colleges, where, by salaries for teachers, on the one hand, and bursaries for the taught, on the other, learning was made more easily accessible; and so a much greater number were allured to the scholarship requisite for the office of a Christian instructor. The necessity for such an artificial encouragement as this, is in itself a strong argument for literary endowments. Without this, we have reason to think, either that the land might have languished under the paucity of its ecclesiastical ministrations; or that Christianity, represented, and feebly represented, by an ignorant and unlettered priesthood, might have been lorded over by an infidel philosophy, and left open to the contempt of general society.

2. It is evident, that the higher the preliminary education for the church was made, the greater must have been the need of endowments; and that, not merely for providing an adequate remuneration to the masters, but by immunities of various sorts attached to them, to induce students to attend in sufficient numbers, notwithstanding the larger amount of fees, and the more lengthened periods of study to which this higher scholarship subjected them. At one time, in Scotland, all the existing encouragements, whether in the shape of bursaries, or honoraries, or gratuitous lodgings, failed to attract so many students as might suffice for the supply of parishes. This is the reason why a constant attendance on the Divinity Hall was dispensed with, and why so many sessions of occasional attendance were sustained, as a sufficient preparatory course for entering upon holy orders. It facilitated the approach of entrants into the ministry; but it did so, by abridging the studies and the sacrifices which they had to make, for the purpose of obtaining the required qualifications. The important thing to be noted here, is the connection that subsists between the character, whether more or less arduous, of the education in colleges, and the consequently smaller or larger number of our clerical aspirants. It is evident, that the longer and more laborious the curriculum is, the fewer will be found to have described it; and conversely. This furnishes a palpable index

E

by which we may judge of the changes that might be made on the state of our academic education. The time has been, when the church, straitened in respect to the number of her licentiates, and at a loss for the supply of her vacant parishes, was forced to let down her requisitions, and, in that proportion, to degrade the scholarship of her clergy. Does not the reverse condition, in which we now are, both permit and justify a reverse process? Might not the fact of a great yearly overplus of probationers, emanating from our colleges upon the ecclesiastical profession, warrant the institution of a more arduous and more expensive course? It would diminish, it is true, the number of our licentiates; but then there is ample room for the diminution. And might not this be turned to the precious account of ordaining a still more laborious preparation for the church, whereby to secure, even for Scotland, the inestimable benefit of a still more lettered and accomplished clergy?

3. It is not our business to theorise on the reasons of that change which has taken place in regard to the number of those who are at present studying for the sacred profession; and whereby there is now an excess, as before there was a deficiency, of licentiates or probationers in our church. It is due, in part, to the augmentation of the church livings, without a proportionate increase in the expense of college education; and also, in part, to a certain influence connected with

the progress of wealth in a country. As society advances, profits decline, and people, in consequence, embark the same money on any given speculation, with the prospect of an inferior return. It would be in the face of all experimental wisdom to deny the reality of this influence even in the business of embarking money on the education of a family. In Scotland, the sum of £200 will be advanced now, for the sake of a smaller return than it would have been a century ago; and, accordingly, if that sum had then been, and still were, the expense of education for any of the learned professions, we should have expected, on that single account, a more crowded attendance at our various universities, even though the pecuniary income in any of the professions had been stationary. The effect, then, must be greatly enhanced, if the outgivings at college bear a smaller proportion now than they did formerly to the earnings whether of the medical profession, or of the law, or of the church. Certain it is, that, in reference to the last of these three professions, the proportion is now utterly reversed between the offices to be filled, and the candidates for these offices. Formerly the vacancies greatly outnumbered the labourers capable of supplying them; and now the labourers greatly outnumber the vacancies. In the Scottish Establishment, there should be somewhat short of thirty nominations to churches in the year,—constituting a demand for licentiates which would be most amply supplied by 200 students of divinity. But three years ago, there were upwards of 700. The profession is greatly overstocked; and so, in fact, are the other two professions of medicine and law,—a state of matters, we repeat, available to the important object of raising the scholarship of them all.

4. It is not for the purpose of reducing the number of competitors that we would beset the entry to the learned professions with additional difficulties. But the present excess of those competitors proves with what safety such difficulties may be imposed. Nor would we impose them for their own sake. The toil and the cost of a more lengthened and laborious attendance at our universities are not desirable in themselves; but the more comprehensive and profounder scholarship to which they are subservient, is highly desirable; and, to the attainment of this object, the present state of matters is convertible. As formerly, we were obliged to let down the system of education, for the purpose of drawing more students to college; so, now that we can afford to have greatly fewer students, we may raise that system. The standard of preparation was lowered when the circumstances of the country required such a facility for the due supply of the learned professions; but now that the facility is such as vastly to have overdone the supply, this is the intimation to us how much the standard of preparation admits of being elevated.

5. The great yearly overplus of students, in Scotland, is a valuable fact, because it at once suggests the expedient by which to reform all that is most objectionable in the peculiarities of our Scottish education, and demonstrates the practicability of that reform.

6. The radical error of our system lies in the too early admittance of our youth to universities. Generally speaking, whether we look to their age or to their acquisitions, they are too soon translated from the pedagogy of a school to the more liberal discipline of a college. The change wanted (and on it every other desirable improvement could be easily suspended), is, that a far higher than their present average scholarship should be exacted from them ere they are admissible as students. As it is, we pass a great deal too early from the treatment of them as boys, to the treatment of them as men. In the majority of cases, they take their departure from the grammar school, without even the first elements of Greek, and without being able to translate extemporaneously the easiest of our Latin authors. It would be well, we repeat, if, ere they could be received into a college *for any professional* object, they had a far higher practical acquaintance with both languages ; and if, by their tried and ascertained expertness in the work of translation, they should evince both that they have a large command of vocables, and that they are thoroughly grounded

in syntax and grammar. But, for this purpose, it seems absolutely indispensable that the period of their boyhood, with its appropriate drudgeries, should be considerably extended. They should be kept at least two or three years longer at drill; whereas at present they are handed over to the professor, before the schoolmaster has finished his work upon them; and, by the existing method of our university tuition, the one is in the worst possible circumstances for executing what the other has left undone. All the vigour and vigilance that can possibly be put forth from the academic chair never will replace the incessant task-work, the close and daily examinations of the school-room. What should be done is, that, ere the university course shall commence, the scholastic course, instead of being cut short, as it now is, should be allowed to attain its proper and adequate completion. It is assuredly in the rudimental part of education that we are defective; and it is in this that we are so much excelled by our southern neighbours. We are weak, throughout, because weak radically. A failure at the root is sure to be indicated by a general sickliness—a lack of strength and stamina, even in spite of that gay and gorgeous efflorescence which disguises the frailty that is underneath. The characteristic freedom, exuberance, and activity of our college system, we hope will remain unchecked and untrammelled; but, certain it is, that these would yield a produce far more enduring, were they grafted on the deep and well-laid foundation of English scholarship.

7. At Berlin, there are institutions termed Gymnasia, of intermediate rank, in point of education, between our high schools and colleges, and through which the students have to pass in their way to that higher order of education which they receive from the faculty professors. In England, too, young men receive a far higher preparation for the university, at the public schools. Now, the thing wanted for Scotland is just some apparatus of equivalent power either to the gymnasia of Prussia, or to the public schools of England ; for, unquestionably, the great defect of our system is, that our youth, by quitting too soon the schoolboy for the student, have not had such thorough exercise and training as is desirable in what we again term the gymnastics of education.

8. There are two simple expedients, by either of which we think that this defect might be remedied.

9. The first is the institution of a more extended grammar school system in each of our university towns. In so far as the Latin is concerned, this could be provided for by the appointment of more classes, with masters who might carry the scholars higher, by several steps, than they now attain in their acquaintance with that tongue. And we should, further, hold a Greek master to be indispensable in each of these seminaries, who might

supersede altogether what is called the first or
public class of Greek in our colleges ;* and who
would certainly be in far better circumstances than
a professor for conducting all the initiatory processes in the acquisition of the language.

10. Or, what we should consider as a still better
arrangement, would be the institution of a Greek
and Latin tutorship in each university, forming an
intermediate passage from our schools to our colleges, and at which the learner should be detained
till he become a fit subject for the higher treatment of a professional course. This would be
tantamount to the gymnasium attached to certain
universities of the continent. Its terms or sessions
might be extended beyond those of the higher
classes; and its teachers, though of distinct rank
and employment from the professors, should, in
reference both to themselves, and their offices, be
regarded as essentially belonging to the university.

11. By the help of one or other of these contrivances, we think that the chief objections to our
present Scottish mode of education might be ob-
viated. To prevent the inconvenience of having
students either so juvenile or so untaught as those
to whom we are often exposed at present, we have
heard it proposed that they should not be admissible to college under a certain specified age. It

---

* Or rather, the present work of the first Greek class, which might then
be appropriated to the present work of the senior class, and so permit a
far higher advancement of our students in Greek language and literature.

would, however, be a better regulation, that they should not be admissible under a certain specified amount of scholarship. The question of their admissibility should be decided, not by their years, but by their acquirements; or by certain definite tests of proficiency which they should be made to undergo in a strict public examination; such, for example, as the execution of certain prescribed versions; the translation of the easier Latin authors *ad aperturam libri;* the translation of assigned passages in some of the more difficult Latin, and easier Greek authors, with a certain allowance of time for preparation ; and, above all, a correct acquaintance with the syntax and grammar of the one language, and such an acquaintance with the other as might be expected from the study of it for at least one, and perhaps two years. At Glasgow, the students, at the commencement of their second, third, and fourth years, are examined on the subjects of their previous education, that their fitness for an ulterior scholarship may be ascertained, ere they are permitted to pass onward in the course. Now, what I should propose is a great initial examination of students at the outset of their university career, or at the commencement of their first session, and that as an indispensable preliminary to their becoming collegians at all. It is on the degree of performance or proficiency executed upon this occasion that the whole of the proposed reformation turns. I should fix a very high standard; and, whenever the youthful aspirant fell short of it, there would be either a grammar school in the university town, or a gymnasium in the university itself, where he could obtain the requisite preparation.

12. But I would not that his attendance either on the one or the other of these institutions were deemed indispensable. His admissibility as a regular student should be made to depend, not on the previous schools which he has attended, but on the previous scholarship which he has acquired. And let him get this scholarship wherever he can find it. It would be well if our provincial schools became so efficient, and the classical teachers at the head of them were so accomplished, as to meet the demand of the new system for higher acquisitions on the part of college entrants. They will not, for a long time, supersede the advantage either of a gymnasium or a completely equipped grammar school at each university seat. But there cannot be imagined a distinction more honourable for any school in the country, than to send up young men to the university, who can stand the arduous initial examination for which it is the office of the gymnasium to prepare them. By this simple device, there might be a wholesome rivalship set agoing, that would give an impulse to elementary or scholastic education all over the land. The ambition, in many towns, and perhaps even in some country parishes, would be to qualify their own scholars

for immediate admission into the faculty classes. And thus, as the fruit of the arrangement which we have ventured to recommend, there would be the almost instant elevation of every college entrant to a far higher grade of scholarship than is now usual; and there would be eventually, in accommodation to this, a far higher style of education in the provincial seminaries of Scotland.*

13. But it is obvious that the whole improvement hangs on the fidelity and strictness with which the initial examination of students is conducted. If once laxity in these respects be admitted, the gymnasium will become a mere piece of useless frame-work; and like many other seemly contrivances of man, be struck with impotency by the faulty administration of it. To secure the faithfulness, then, of the examination, men of rival and opposite interests should be admitted to a voice in it. The tutors of the gymnasium, whose classes might receive augmentation from the number of defeated candidates, should have a seat in the board of examinators. Even eminent school-masters from the country might be invited to assist at this grave and formidable trial. And this very attention should be conferred on the one side, and would be felt on the other, as a flattering reward for the assiduity and success wherewith these meritorious men had, in their respective nurseries

---

* See Note F, Appendix.

of scholarship, raised so many into a fit state for
being transplanted into the higher field of a university. It would, further, be well, if, on the occasion
of this great anniversary, the colleges sent corresponding members to each other, even as the synods
of the church do. For there is an interest which
each college has in admitting with greater facility
than the others, and against which a check ought to
be provided. But far the most precious fruit of this
attendant publicity, and pomp and circumstance,
would be the stimulus that it should give to all the
seminaries where the preparatory education was
carried on; and the high feats of prowess in scholarship to which it should urge every youthful aspirant
in the prospect of that exhibition which was before
him. It would be no small advantage, that it
marked the strength of that barrier which had to
be forced ere the entry was made on a higher education. The greater the appearance which the
wall of separation between schools and colleges
made in the public eye, the more strenuous would
be the preparation in the lower, and the more sustained and lofty, it is hoped, would be the state of
the scholarship in the higher seminaries.

14. We prefer a gymnasium in the university to
an extended grammar school in the university
town; and in the gymnasium we should like also a
mathematical tutor, as well as a Greek and a Latin
one, in order to repair our great inferiority in
mathematical science to the nations of the conti-

nent. It is desirable, we think, that, previous to their first year at college, students should acquire all that they now learn at the professor's first mathematical class. Suppose that they have mastered the first six books of Euclid, with plane trigonometry, and algebra up to quadratic equations, before entering the class of the faculty professor of mathematics, this would enable him to carry them to such heights of science, as, under the present system, are completely unattainable during the season of attendance at the university. Were this arrangement adopted, there behoved, of course, at the great initiatory trial of college entrants, to be a mathematical as well as a classical examination.

15. The expense of such an institution might not go beyond £300 a-year for each university. In the smaller universities, one tutor would probably suffice for each of the departments, and the annual salary required for each might not exceed £100. In the larger universities, a greater number of tutors might be required, but their smaller salaries would be greatly more than compensated by the fees of their larger attendance.*

16. They only, however, who propose to study

---

* The very high-state of education, both in the High School of Edinburgh and at the New Academy, would of course lessen the demand for instruction in a gymnasium there, though we do not think that it should supersede the institution of one, unless the masters of these seminaries were admitted to, and had a voice at the initial examination.

for one or other of the learned professions, should
be subject to the examination in question. All
the classes should be as open as they are now, to
the general public; and any new regulation connected with a gymnasium, or qualifications to be
ascertained by an initiatory trial, should be con-
fined to the students of law, medicine, and theology. The ultimate object of such a guardianship
as that proposed should be, to elevate the learned
professions, and not to intercept the approaches to
college of those who resort to it purely for the
sake of instruction, and without any professional
view. It is enough that for the aspirants to any
learned profession, the examination at entry on the
studies which qualify for it, should be held indispensable; and that the certificate of having passed
this examination should be required along with
the certificates of attendance on the prescribed
classes. In this way, literature is as freely dispensed as before to those with whom literature is
the sole object; while lawyers, physicians, and
clergymen are restricted to that course which secures for them a higher education, and so secures
for the land still more accomplished functionaries
than before.

17. It is obvious, that under the proposed arrangement, there would, for a time at least, be
fewer students than at present: and that, because
of the more lengthened and expensive course which
they should have to undergo. A higher prepara-

tory education, whether at the gymnasium or at schools, might, in the case of theological students, be tantamount to a prolongation of their attendance at college of from eight to ten years. This behoved to operate as a check upon their numbers; and it is well that so large a reduction of numbers can be afforded without at all hazarding the adequate supply of church vacancies. The existing overplus of students of divinity is often spoken of with regret. But it will become a matter of gratulation, when turned to a purpose so valuable as that of refining and raising to a still higher point of elevation, both the general and the professional literature of clergymen.

18. But with fewer students, and no increase either of fees or salaries, the professors would sustain a reduction of their income. This seems to furnish an irresistible argument in behalf, not only of our existing, but even of larger endowments. Are the teachers to descend to a lower status; and that by the very arrangement of which the main purpose is to elevate the taught to a higher scholarship? No way appears to us of rightly adjusting any scheme for a more arduous university course, that does not enhance the necessity for endowments. We shall in vain look for this improvement as the fruit of a spontaneous demand by the public for a higher education. This higher education must be made imperative, by a statute of apprenticeship; and whenever it is so, there will be,

for a time at least, a diminished attendance upon colleges. It is to compensate this, that there ought to be an increase of revenue provided for professors from some source or other,—from salaries or fees. The process is analogous to that which we have conceived for parish schools (chap. i. 14, 15.)

19. It is farther obvious, that, by exacting from students at their entry upon college, higher initial qualifications than they have at present, we elevate the work not merely of the language professors, but of all the professors of all the sciences. They would have to deal with more advanced pupils in each of the classes. They would have to accommodate the style of their tuition to understandings more on the eve of manhood. They would have to prepare a more substantial repast for the hardier and more exercised intellects of those who listened to them. There is great discomfort to a public instructor when haunted by the suspicion that he is above the level of those whom he addresses. But the discomfort is far more painful, when humbled by the opposite suspicion that he is beneath that level. It is thus that a higher set of pupils act by a sort of moral compulsion on the professor in raising the whole tone and character of his preparations; and he is tempted to higher walks than before by the feeling that now he will be followed by the intelligent sympathy of those with whom he can safely hold more lofty and scientific converse.

Under this arrangement, the reproach which has
been cast on our Scottish universities, of dealing in
metaphysics and all other sorts of adventurous
speculation with boys of fifteen, would in time be
wiped away. When once our classes were furnished with students both more advanced in age
and more elevated in acquirements, this incongruity would no longer exist. It would be competent for a professor to conduct such students to
the very altitudes of his subject; and thus to accomplish that two-fold service which Scottish professors have often rendered, who, while engaged
in the work of original preparation for the class-
room, have, at the same time, pushed forward the
limits of discovery in their respective sciences.

20. There ought to be a distinction observed between the work of a professor and that of a schoolmaster; and the proposed gymnasium may be regarded as marking the transition space, or as a
broad line of demarcation between them. At the
admission of our young men to college, the pedagogical treatment should give way to the professorial; and the wide difference between these
two should be felt even in those languages, the
study of which is prosecuted for at least two years
in the greater number of our universities. This
difference, we think, might be illustrated by a
comparison between the work of him who, in the
reading of a Greek or Latin author, is obliged to

F

have frequent recourse to his grammar and diction-
ary; and the work of him who, able to translate
without the necessity of constant appeal to these,
can now discriminate the peculiarities of the writer,
and feel the force and beauty of his expressions,
and appreciate the sentiments which he utters,
and treasure up the information which he affords.
The business of a schoolmaster is to superintend
the former of these two works. The business of
a professor is to superintend the latter of them.
There must of course be a good deal of translation
performed before the professor; and this of itself
will help both to keep up and to extend the practical acquaintance of his students with the language which he teaches. But with their now
fuller command of its vocables, and their now
greater intimacy with its syntax and structure, he
will have more time and liberty for his own proper
office, which is to point out the niceties of its
idiom and dialect,—to trace the law of its various
metrical constructions,—to mark the characteristics and the felicities of its different writers,—to
exercise the taste and discernment of his pupils on
the eloquence and poetry of the ancients,—to illustrate the passages which are read in the class-room
by a reference to the history, customs, and locali-
ties of Greece or Rome,—and to unfold the philosophy of grammar, whereby the phenomena of
speech are examined in connection with the laws

and the processes of human thought.* To guide, in short, his disciples along the higher walks of literature and refined criticism, constitutes the proper business of a professor; and in the prosecution of this object, care should be taken that much translation be gone through, and many versions executed. In the examination of these last, again, it is the part of the schoolmaster to attend to the fidelity of the rendering; but it should be that of the professor to attend both to its fidelity and its elegance.

21. But if, even in the teaching of languages, there is room for the distinction between a pedagogical and a professorial treatment of this work, much more does the distinction admit of being verified in the teaching of the sciences. At the outset of a mathematical course of study, it seems advisable that each student should be tasked, and tried with every demonstration in the plane geometry of Euclid, and made to resolve a variety of examples in all the cases of plane trigonometry. But it is not therefore necessary, or even desirable, that he should be followed thus closely, through

---

* It is much to be desired, that Dr. John Hunter of St. Andrews, who stands unrivalled in this high walk of investigation, would favour the world with those original views, which, for upwards of half a century, he has been in the habit of delivering from the chair. As specimens of his characteristic excellence, the reader may consult the notes to his editions of various classics, his treatise on the Tenses of the Latin Verb, appended to his edition of Ruddiman's Rudiments, and his Essay on the Greek δε, &c. published in the Philosophical Transactions of Edinburgh.

the subsequent and more advanced stages of the
science. Let us suppose him to have been thoroughly schooled and exercised in the elementary
mathematics, and that then, with higher preparation, and a more mature understanding than at present, he passes onward to the collegiate method of
studying this branch of education, which obtains
in Scotland. He might be one in a class of fifty,
or even of a hundred, and yet make substantial
progress notwithstanding. He cannot, it is true,
be examined on every demonstration; yet he must
prepare for the chance of being examined on it,
for he knows not but that he may be named for
that purpose. After having undergone all the
previous gymnastics through which we suppose him
to have passed, he is fit surely for reading intelligently over by himself a treatise on conic sections.
Much more might he follow intelligently the lucu-
brations of a master who demonstrates and ex-
plains every proposition, and who has every demonstration repeated to him by one or other of
the students. That he may be the student called
upon, operates as a stimulus both to his attention
in the class-room, and to his busy preparation out
of doors. Add to this, the prescribed exercises
which he may be frequently required to perform,
and which in no instance can escape the observation of the professor, who, it may be farther observed, will find no difficulty in giving to each
student his relative place in the scale of merit and

estimation. The pupils of a college-class in Scotland, are not acted upon by that compulsion which is proper to boys; but they may be fully acted upon by that higher and more generous compulsion which is proper to young men. The great thing to be desired for giving effect to our system, is, that they shall have enough outgrown their boyhood, and have approached sufficiently near to manhood, before the higher studies are entered upon. After which there is every security for their making a sound progress in these studies, inasmuch as that all who will to make that progress may make it: and, in fact, it is quite practicable, by exercises and examinations together, to bring the talent and proficiency of each fully out both to the view of the professor and of his class. The merits of not one of the students need remain unknown. The able and attentive may have the opportunity of signalising themselves throughout the session by their masterly appearances, whether in oral or written demonstrations. Even they to whom mathematics are a drudgery, have all the impulse to exertion, which lies in the approbation of their teacher, and the awarded respect of their fellow-students. * Certain, too, it is, that they who

---

* In the English colleges, there is great efficacy ascribed to their prizes. In our own colleges, all that is needed is an hour for examination in each class,—and numerously attended as many of them are, there would be presented at least the weekly, if not daily opportunity of such distinguished exhibitions, on the part of the ablest students, as should carry in them all the moral efficacy of a prize.

have come forth from the gymnasium smitten with
a taste for the sciences, and endowed with an intellect which triumphs in the difficulties with which
it has to contend, and is regaled with its success in
surmounting them, might follow their professor,
without the failure of a single step, to the very
highest of his lessons, even though he should carry
them to the utmost verge of our present discoveries.

22. They who conceive of the Scotch university
system as hollow and inefficient throughout, overlook the distinction between that treatment which
is right for boys, and that which is right for men.
Surely if a full-grown man may, in virtue of his
present maturity and previously acquired scholarship, read with perfect intelligence the most arduous book in mathematics or morals, though
altogether left to himself,—then, the nearer a
learner is to this maturity and manhood, the more
independent he is of aid and superintendence on
the part of a living master. He may require this
aid to a certain degree, just as he might require
the help of a commentary to throw light on some
difficult text. But just as the commentary should
be more or less copious, according to the various
ages or acquirements of the reader, so ought the
expositions of the teacher to be more or less full,
and the examinations to be more or less frequent,
according to the advancement of his pupils. There
is in this matter a keeping between the age and

the regimen,—a time when the puerile discipline may be relaxed with safety and advantage, before it is given up altogether. There is as much one educational treatment for a youth of twenty, and another for a boy of fifteen, as there is one treatment for a boy of ten years of age, and another for a child of five. Because the class-room of an English tutor, with its perpetual task-work, and its close over-hanging vigilance, is the best adapted for youth of a lower age; it follows not that the lecture-room of a Scotch Professor, even though the practicks of education obtain there in a far less degree, is not the best adapted for youth of a higher age. Our great error is, that we admit students too soon into the lecture-room,—not that our university system is not the best, which can be made to bear on a certain period in the growth and development of the human intellect, but that we make it to bear on a wrong period, on a period immature for the application of it. But the way to amend this is to alter the period, and not to overturn the system,—not to sink the collegiate into the scholastic, but, preserving them distinct, to take care that the scholastic course shall be thoroughly described, before the collegiate course is entered upon.

23. Nevertheless we most willingly allow that we are deficient in the practicks of education. We would have these admitted more largely even into our highest classes. Not that we would give

up the hour which at present is devoted almost
exclusively to the lecture of the professor; but it
would be an improvement, if in each class there
was another hour for examinations and exercises.
With this supplement, the Scottish system should
remain untouched; and professors should be left
as heretofore to their own independent views, and
their own original style of treatment and preparation in all the sciences;—not tied down to the
order and the lessons of an antiquated text-book,*
but at liberty to change their instructions with the
light and spirit of the age, and themselves in the
advanced position of men who, after having tra-
versed all the doctrines of our existent philosophy,
can both enrich it and widen its domain by discoveries and doctrines of their own.

24. It would be no subversion of this professorial
method of teaching, but an improvement of it, to
superadd the stimulus of a great public examination
at the end of each session, in every way as sifting
and severe as those which are held in the English
universities, at the dispensation of honours, and
affording the same tests of high proficiency in the
various sciences as are required at our sister institutions in mathematics and the ancient languages.
We maintain, that, by our peculiar methods, students can be effectually prepared for such a trial;
and that, from the lecture-rooms of our Scottish

---

* See Note G, Appendix.

Professors, there might issue youths as thoroughly accomplished in the principles of the ethical and intellectual philosophy, in political economy, and the various branches of a theological education, as if they had been made to undergo that more elaborate distillation which is imaged to take place in the tutors' class-rooms of Oxford and Cambridge.

25. There is doubtless a certain style of close and almost compulsory tuition by which every doctrine of a text-book might be infused into the scholar's mind, and which can be better accomplished by a Fellow, in his chamber, with a few pupils, than by a Professor, in his lecture-room, with many. But then, however needed by boys, it is not needed by young men who have outgrown their boyhood. For example, a class might thus be most minutely and thoroughly lessoned in every chapter and paragraph of Paley's Moral Philosophy: and yet we are confident that, by the ordinary collegiate methods of Scotland, and more especially if an hour of examination were superadded to the hour of lecturing, a tenfold greater number of youths could not only be instructed, but soundly instructed, and that within half a-year, not in the doctrines of this book only, but in all the doctrines of any worth or prominency which are to be found in the most distinguished works on ethical science. In that space of time, the professor could take a wide compass over the whole literature of his subject; and he could deliver

with fulness and effect all the truths of permanent importance which have been expounded by our best writers, from Bacon and Butler, to Brown and Dugald Stewart of our own day; and he could make full exposure of the scepticisms and the infidel sophistries by which the orthodox system of morals has been assailed; and he could sit in judgment on all his predecessors; and without either trampling on that which is precious, or going wildly astray after the novelties of wayward speculation, he could nevertheless cast the science in the mould of his own understanding, and transmute it into his own language, and throw all the freshness of an original interest over the lessons of his course; and with these lessons he could thoroughly imbue the great majority of his pupils, traversing along with them the whole length and breadth of his department, and giving them we are sure a far greater amount of instruction than they ever could acquire by conning over the dicta of any single author in the pages of an established text-book. For giving effect to this high professorial mode of teaching, all that we require is a sufficient age for our pupils. This is the great reformation wanted; and not that we should exchange the methods of Smith, and Stewart, and Playfair and Jardine, and Black, for the mere pedagogy of the English colleges.

26. It is just because the preparatory schooling is so complete in England, that there the peda-

gogical method admits of being relaxed in the universities; and our professorial method might with all the more safety be substituted in its room. And it is just because our preparatory schooling is so very deficient, that the professorial style of instruction wherewith it is instantly followed up, lies open to the charge of being so very preposterous and premature. There is thus a perversity in each of the two systems; and it would not be the way to amend either of them that it should be run entirely into the other. The danger to be apprehended is, lest in the work of amelioration which has begun with the colleges of Scotland, it should be proposed to sink the business of a professor into that of a schoolmaster; whereas the only right way of proceeding would be to provide that the schoolmaster finish his work, ere the higher task of the professor shall be entered upon. We trust that the main characteristics of our Scottish system, instead of being subverted, will be kept inviolate, and that our professorial method of tuition will not be done away, but only provided with a good basis of English pedagogy.

27. This being provided, we are satisfied that our Scottish system might be compared most advantageously with the system which obtains in the universities of England. There we behold the strictly scholastic method kept up often beyond the age of majority, in the two departments of mathematics and the classics. And the main

strength of teachers and pupils being thus centered upon one or two subjects, there arises, as we might expect, the natural consequence of a greater amount of high proficiency in these, than is generally to be found in the seminaries which have adopted a more comprehensive scheme of education. Yet, we cannot for a moment doubt, that, from the latter seminaries, if under the conduct of able professors in all the sciences, a far greater produce of usefulness might be thrown off upon society. All that is wanted for this is the exaction of higher qualifications at the outset of the university career; that the faculties of our students may be enough expanded for the lessons of a sublime or arduous philosophy; and that, although beyond the coercion which would absolutely force a daily preparation for each, there may, from the single circumstance of their age, be a sufficient guarantee in the power of manly and liberal inducements alone for at least a large proportion of them in every class entering fully and vigorously into the spirit and studies of the course. To us it is inconceivable how accomplished linguists and mathematicians, and economists, and moralists, and theologians, and chemists, and naturalists, can fail of being formed under an arrangement like this; or wherein lies the mysterious inaptitude of such an apparatus for the effective conveyance of full and substantial instruction in all the branches of science and literature. It will therefore scarcely admit of a question, by which of the two systems of education a greater service is rendered to the community,—whether by universities that send forth many of their sons thoroughly schooled, in mathematics and the ancient languages, but in these two branches of education alone; or by universities that send forth fewer so well accomplished in these, but that make up for this defect by sending forth a few who have made eminent proficiency in each of the sciences, and many besides, who, though not beyond a respectable mediocrity in any of the separate departments of human knowledge, yet, in the description of their college course, have acquired a general intellectual cultivation, which is thereby largely diffused throughout the higher and middling classes of society.

28. The comparison between the two systems may be made thus. Only the few, by dint of surpassing strength and genius, are fitted to extend the boundaries of any of the sciences. The many never realise this glory, and yet, they receive incalculable good from studies in which they make considerable advances, although immeasurably distanced therein by those of colossal mind, who are destined to outpeer all their fellows, and to be the luminaries of their age. To receive benefit from a science, it is not necessary that one should attain the station of a master or a discoverer. There is a scholarship far short of this, which may so grace

and inform the mind as to be of inestimable worth to its possessor. We even think that the spread of this more moderate proficiency among hundreds, is of greater use and importance to society than would be the elevation of half a dozen to superlative rank and accomplishment in learning. But both are best; and we most willingly admit that it would be a serious deduction from the usefulness of a college, if it failed in either one or other of these services.

29. By this distinction between the few highly eminent, and the many merely respectable scholars, we shall be the better enabled to set the English and Scottish university modes of education fairly against each other. In regard to the first class of scholars, the highly eminent, it is evident, that, under either mode, there is enough of practical teaching for the development of that special capacity and power to which their aptitude for eminence is owing. There may be more of task-work and lessoning in the southern than in the northern colleges; but it is not by the mere dint and quantity of lessoning that genius is created, although a certain amount of it be necessary for the excitement of genius to those spontaneous and self-sustained efforts by which mainly its future triumphs are achieved. Now, we contend that such an amount of lessoning is to be had in the colleges of Scotland—as much of it, indeed, in every department of education as will set every

student having the requisite taste and talent which
may qualify him for eminence in that department
most prosperously agoing. Let the bent of his
inclinations and energies be towards philology, or
belles lettres, or mathematics, or physics, or ethics,
or economical science, he comes in contact with
enough of his favourite subject for awakening the
kindred inspiration, and enough, too, of practical
guidance for directing him on that path of study,
in which, if he be gifted with original and inventive
faculties, his conceptions may ripen into immortal
authorship. Only grant, then, that those minds
of surpassing force and fire, which need but the
touch of some congenial excitement, that they may
kindle into the luminaries of their age,—only
grant, in regard to such minds, that they may be
as effectually ignited at a Scotch as at an English
college; and then we ask, in behalf of the former
institution, whether it is not better that all the
various sciences should be presented to the various
taste and intellect of its students, than that its
whole discipleship should consist in the exclusive
and incessant appliance of but two subjects or two
sciences? Is it not better for the country, that,
at the great fountain-heads of its literature, there
should be rendered a supply of human knowledge
in all its branches; and that altogether, there
should, in the wide range of its professorships, be
as many affinities provided as might suit the peculiar aptitude and disposition of every genius? In

this way each master spirit is furnished with its own proper science; and each science, in the encyclopedia of human learning, acts by its own magnetic charm on every spirit that is kindred to itself. There is thus a far greater amount of superlative talent enlisted in the service of philosophy, and that not in but one or two of its branches, but in all the most important diversities of human study and human speculation. We do not lose, under this generalised system of education, the services of those, who, in virtue of their peculiar mental conformation, are signally and specially qualified, either in the ancient languages to shed an original light over the walks of criticism, or in the mathematics to extend the resources of the science, and open up new tracks of investigation. And additionally to these, we secure minds of another conformation for the like high service in other sciences. We supply each first-rate genius with the theme which he is best adapted to perfect or to adorn; and, instead of only sending forth men fitted more thoroughly to explore the classics, or more widely to extend the mathematics than before; we overspread the entire field of human knowledge, with labourers, each qualified to make original contributions in his own department, and collectively to enrich and to enlarge not one or two, but all the provinces of learning.

30. But the comparison we are making has hitherto respected chiefly those who are capable

of reaching the loftiest scholarship. Another comparison has yet to be made in reference to those who, though far short of eminence like this, yet acquire at universities the polish, and the information, and the disciplined intellect, and the certain cast of mental strength and superiority which are generally attendant on the pursuits of literature, even although the specific acquisitions do not amount to more than what may be termed a respectable scholarship. And the question is, whether it is better that the acquisitions to be obtained at our seminaries should be restricted to one or two, or should be extended to all the sciences. In other words, whether among a thousand students who have reached proficiency in one or other of the classes, it is better for the society wherein they mingle in future life, that one half of this number should be good linguists, and another half good mathematicians, or that they should be still more subdivided, so as to afford a smaller number of good linguists and good mathematicians, and to leave a surplus, out of which there may be drawn so many good theologians, and good naturalists, and good economists, and good chemists, and good or tolerable adepts in all the branches of literature and philosophy. Is it not better that there should be all these varieties of acquirement and mental cultivation corresponding to the varieties of truth and nature? For the general intelligence of a people, is it not a good thing that there should at least be some, however few, who are intelligent in each one branch of human knowledge that can be specified? Is it desirable for a nation, that its whole literary public should be made up of mere philologists and mere geometers? If not, can that institution be said to fulfil the proper end of a *university* which, instead of furnishing society with proficients in every kind of scholarship, deals exclusively in the manufacture of but two species of literary men? When truth and nature offer such manifold varieties of mental food, is a university, which dispenses so limited a number of these varieties, and withholds all the rest, in keeping either with the powers of man, or with the objects of that theatre by which he is surrounded?* Would it not, then, by a more comprehensive scheme of education, adapt itself more both to the diverse exigencies of human life, and to the diverse appetencies of the human intellect?

31. But we are now proceeding on the supposition, that they who describe the curriculum of a Scottish college, make proficiency only in one branch of education. Certain it is, that, in the majority of instances, there is one favourite science in which each student makes his greatest profi-

---

* We are sensible, while making this comparison between two systems, that neither of them is exemplified, whether in England or Scotland, to the full: that, on the one hand, in our universities the complement of sciences is not altogether made up; and that, on the other hand, along with the regular courses of Oxford and Cambridge, there are public lectures delivered on a variety of subjects.

ciency. But, along with this, he very commonly receives a certain infusion of the other sciences; and the various faculties of his mind are exercised and improved by the various studies in which he is engaged,—as his taste in the study of languages and belles lettres, his reason in the study of mathematics, his power of internal reflection in the study of human nature, and his power of analysis, by which he elicits principles from the complex phenomena presented to him, when studying the doctrines of economical science or the relations of civil society. Besides all this, too, a mind which thus diversifies its acquisitions finds itself in a state of completer adjustment with the actual diversities of that scene over which man expatiates, and in which he has a part to perform. It is more cast, as it were, in the mould of universal truth, and becomes more nearly a mirror of that divine workmanship which is itself the mirror of that manifold wisdom wherewith all things have been created. It surely tends to grace and dignify an individual, and not to derogate from his honour, when it is said of him that he has a mind stored with various information. This, doubtless, is a better and higher accomplishment than to be a mere linguist, or a mere mathematician, or, indeed, a mere proficient in any single department of knowledge,—whose one exclusive *forte* or faculty confers little or no illustration on its possessor, unless in those rare cases where it elevates him to the rank of a master and discoverer in science. The man of blended and comprehensive acquirements bids fairer to acquit himself well, both in the business of life and the converse of society; and such acquirements can more readily be had in describing the round of that varied education for which we are now contending.

32. We have thought it necessary to say thus much on our Scottish collegiate methods of instruction, in the conviction, that by means of some very practicable improvements, the objections which have been charged against them may be fully done away. It has been charged upon our universities, that there is a want of what the French would call *approfondisement* amongst us; that we offer nought but the sketches of a varied and agreeable, but withal meagre, philosophy; that even when the course of some occasional professor is profound as well as brilliant, such as, most undoubtedly, was that of Reid, and Brown, and Dr. Adam Smith, yet, from the very bare cognizance which is taken of the pupils, there is a want, at all events, of complete and substantial scholarship among them; and that thus, from the colleges of the north there emanates a whole host of pretenders, who, though abundantly versant in the phraseology of science, have made no careful and elaborate search into its principles. We admit that at present, and more especially in our higher classes, there is a lack of sufficient inspection over the progress of our students. But this could easily be remedied to all the extent that is desirable, after which, we only require the at-

tendance of more advanced students, in order that they may be made as expert and as erudite in the modern philosophy as our English neighbours are in the ancient languages. The college apparatus of Scotland is fully competent to such an effect— to the effect of nurturing a hardy race of severe and sound thinkers in every walk of human speculation—men of depth and substance and firm staple —and of far purer and wiser aim than to shine forth in the tiny lustre of those slender and superficial, but withal plausible accomplishments, which have been said by our contemptuous friends in the south to constitute all the philosophy of our nation.

33. But we must return from this digression, yet not without deducing' from it what we have ever held to be a valid, and, indeed, an incontrovertible reason, in behalf of literary endowments. For giving such efficacy to our college system, as may place above, or even put it on a level, in point of utility, with the university system of England, it seems indispensable that our students should be greatly more advanced, both in age and in acquisitions, than on the average they are at present. But such a reformation would obviously lessen the number of pupils, and so proportionally lessen the revenues of the professors. Or, in other words, that change which imposes upon them the task of a far more arduous preparation for the lessons of a now more arduous philosophy, is, at the same time,

a change which, if not followed up by any compensation, must oblige them to forego a portion of their emoluments, and so to descend to a lower status in society. This compensation is only to be found, either in larger fees, or in larger endowments. And if it be indeed true that professors are already sufficiently low in the scale of society,—if these public functionaries have been immeasurably left behind in the growing opulence of all the classes in the state,—if, as it unquestionably holds in the provincial universities, the masters there are scarcely enabled, even with the severest struggle, to support the establishments, or to maintain the appearance of gentlemen,—then the cause of endowments is that of pure science and of lofty sentiment, however maligned it may have been by a spurious or mistaken patriotism.

34. The pending experiment in London is well fitted to manifest the principles of this subject. The university there is to be slenderly endowed, and the main security of the professors for a revenue is to be laid on the spontaneous demand for education. And there will be no statutes of apprenticeship to compel an attendance upon its classes; so that, at the outset, it will have nothing to look to for its support, but the prevailing taste for literature and philosophy in the metropolis. What we should anticipate, in these circumstances, is a larger attendance, at the first, from the force and attraction of novelty, but which will afterwards

subside, to the discouragement perhaps, though
not, we trust, to the utter despair of those who at
present are most sanguine in their hopes of a great
coming enlargement both of light and of liberty
from this patriotic institution. We do apprehend
for this seminary of magnificent promise, the mor-
tifying experience of a native sluggishness and
apathy on the part of the city families, ere a higher
taste shall be created among them, and there shall
be excited a more adequate demand for the attainments of a severe and exalted scholarship. But
for such an elevation of the general taste of these
families, the infancy of this noble undertaking
must be cherished to the uttermost; and it may
even need the strenuous perseverance of years,
ere it shall be fostered into the conclusive state of
a secure and lasting establishment. And after all,
we fear that, for the upholding of its prosperity,
there must be a perpetual compromise between
pure science, on the one hand, and the popular
taste upon the other. There will need to be a
half-way meeting between them,—a descent on
the part of philosophy, from its own proper level,
in order to draw the general mind upward to at
least a higher level than it before occupied. The
service is invaluable; but a sacrifice must be made
for the performance of it. The otherwise dull
and didactic course must be enlivened by a thousand expedients not altogether in keeping with the
dignity of stern and high intellect—as an occasional

flash of eloquenee, though somewhat misplaced amid the abstruser doctrines which it is intended to relieve; or the glare of showy experiments, though not the best fitted for the manifestation of principle; or an abatement from the rigour of demonstrations, without which the judgment is left unsatisfied. In a word, effect must be consulted to the uttermost; and the dread is, lest the high interests of truth and reason should suffer by it. The seminary must adjust itself to the taste and demand of society; and may not, in fact, be able to get on without a certain dash of that empiricism which both tarnishes the honours, and deteriorates the firm staple of philosophy. It will do incalculable good in its sphere; although, far above it, there should be the upper spheres of chaste, and lofty, and ethereal intellect. It is well that the citizens of our land should be provided with as much light as they will receive and pay for; but that is no reason why the savans of our land should not be provided with a purer and a higher light, even though it should fetch no price in the general market. And it is just because it fetches no price that, unless upholden in another way, it will inevitably expire. On the principle of demand and supply, there may be the spread of a popular philosophy; but if left exclusively to this, there may be the utter disappearance of a transcendant philosophy from our nation. We therefore trust, that, for science in its best and loftiest character, there will ever subsist its present hospitable asylum in the old attic retreats of Oxford and Cambridge, where it may continue to flourish as heretofore in the shade and under the shelter of college endowments. We feel no doubt that thence will still issue forth the largest proportion of our most precious and enduring literature; and that, whatever the light may be which shall radiate from more modern seminaries, it will, generally speaking, be found that, in light of superior purity and permanence, the existing universities both of England and Scotland shall greatly overpass them.*

35. We shall be greatly misunderstood, however, if it be thought that we hold the proposed university of the metropolis in light estimation. It will achieve a mighty service if it but elevate the middling classes of that immense city to a higher grade in the scale of mental cultivation, even although in science and scholarship it should come far short of the endowed colleges. But what confers its chief interest on this projected seminary is, that it will act upon these colleges by a most

---

* The celebrated Lacroix of Paris, teaches a class of the higher mathematics, where he is often not attended by more than eight students. If he furnish his country with that number of accomplished mathematicians every year, he renders back to it a sufficient value for all that he receives in the shape of salary. But how could such a class be sustained by fees alone? It is proposed, we understand, that the salaries of the higher professors in the London University shall be paid from the overplus of those fees which are paid for the more popular classes. This is a truly interesting experiment; and every enlightened friend of his species will rejoice in the success of it.

wholesome reflex influence. The very dread of being outrivalled will force them to bestir themselves; and, in whatever degree they may have heretofore been the dormitories of literature, we know not a more effectual device than a great popular institution like this, for awakening their latent energies. The very dismay and jealousy wherewith it is regarded by the dignitaries of our established system, are the best guarantees of a coming renovation. Professors will be aroused from their indolence, and patrons be ashamed of that vile prostitution by which the chairs of philosophy have been trafficked, and bestowed at the bidding of an ignoble politics. For reasons on which we have now abundantly insisted, we conceive that, in an endowed, there is a better mechanism than in an unendowed college, for working off the products of science and sound literature. But if there be a virtue in the worse mechanism to stimulate the better mechanism, and set it more actively agoing; then to the former really, though indirectly, we may have to attribute the high service of raising and sustaining the character of philosophy in our land. It is not difficult to reconcile our preference for endowed universities to the pleasure wherewith we contemplate the rise of a great popular university in the midst of them. The one sentiment is truly the effect of the other. The recent institution will never, we think, outstrip the older ones; but it will urge them onward, so that they shall be perpetually ahead of itself. It will be the impellent cause for advancing and elevating the tone of science, even though a high toned science may never be dispensed from its own lecture-rooms. It will work its greatest good through the medium of Oxford and Cambridge; and, in their ostensible triumph, and its own apparent defeat and inferiority, will an intelligent observer recognize the most substantial proof of the great service it shall have achieved for the nation.

36. There is a bigotry on the side of endowed seminaries which leads those whom it actuates to be jealous of popular institutions. And, on the other hand, there is a generous feeling towards these institutions, which is often accompanied with a certain despite towards the endowed and established seminaries. We think that a more comprehensive consideration of the actings and reactings which take place in society, should serve to abate the heats of this partizanship; and, that what in one view is regarded as the conflict of jarring and hostile elements, should, in another, be rejoiced in as a luminous concourse of influences, tending to accomplish the grand and beneficent result of an enlightened nation. It is just because we wish so well to colleges, that we hail the prosperity of mechanic institutions. The latter will never outrun the former, but so stimulate them onwards, that the literature of our higher classes

shall hold the same relative advancement and superiority as before over the literature of our artizans. It will cause no derangement and no disproportion. The light which shall then over-spread the floor of the social edifice, will only cause the lustres which are in the higher apartments to blaze more gorgeously. The basement of the fabric will be greatly more elevated, yet without violence to the symmetry of the whole architecture; for the pinnacles and upper stories of the building will rise as proudly and as gracefully as ever above the platform which sustains them. There is in-definite room in truth and science for an ascending movement, and the taking up of higher positions: and if, in virtue of a popular philosophy now taught in schools of art, we are to have more let-tered mechanics, this will be instantly followed up by a higher philosophy in colleges than heretofore; and in virtue of which we shall also have a more ac-complished gentry, a more intellectual parliament, a more erudite clergy, and altogether a greater force and fulness of mind throughout all the de-partments of the commonwealth. The whole of society will ascend together, and therefore without disturbance, to the relation of its parts. But, in every stage of this progress, the endowed colleges will continue to be the highest places of intellect; the country's richest lore: and its most solid and severest philosophy will always be found in them.

CHAPTER III.

ON CHURCH ENDOWMENTS.*

1. THE argument in behalf of endowments seems to stand on the same footing with Christian as with common education. In the one case it is founded on the languor of the intellectual appetite; so that ignorance, if left to itself, will not, by any spontaneous effort of its own, go in quest of instruction, or provide the effectual means by which it may be supplied to the extent that is desirable. In the other case, there may be alleged the languor of the moral or the spiritual appetite; so that irreligion, if left to itself, will not originate the movement by which it may be brought into contact with that ministration which is best suited to it. In both cases, the subject to be dealt with must be addressed by an application from without. It must be treated aggressively. And, in like manner, as schools have to be raised, and teacher's salaries to be provided for every little district of the land, ere the inert mass can be thoroughly pervaded with scholarship—so we fear that, with-

---

* The argument in behalf of an endowed and established church is more fully expounded by the author in a former work—entitled, " The Christian and Civic Economy of Large Towns." See Vol. I. Chap. III.

out a like provision of churches and beneficed churchmen to preach in them, the vast majority of our land would be left without the reach of gospel calls, or gospel opportunities.

2. The experiment of leaving religion without a religious establishment, has been tried on a large scale in America: and it is much to be wished that we had thorough statistical information from that country as to the results of it. It is not enough to be told of the revivals which have taken place in that part of the world; nor yet of the many churches, with their full attendance, in certain towns or even provinces of that immense territory. These, although of an imposing magnitude when stated absolutely, may yet be of small comparative amount to the exigencies of the whole population. And besides, in most of the Northern States, at least till very lately, there was an ecclesiastical system altogether tantamount to an establishment—a revenue exacted and set aside by law for the maintenance of a clergy, though a clergy not of one but of various denominations. It has often been affirmed, that to this arrangement the people of New England stood indebted for the evident superiority of their moral and religious habits over those of the southern and middle states. We have further heard, that in New Hampshire the law of a compulsory provision for the teachers of Christianity has recently been abolished—and with this effect, that, in many in-

stances, when a chapel has become vacant by the death of the incumbent, his place has not been supplied; and the district which enjoyed his services, now left without any Sabbath ministrations whatever, gives melancholy attestation to the native listlessness and unconcern of its families. Certain it is, that in other places of the Union, even in those which have been settled so long, as now to have reached a high state both of wealth and population, there is abundant proof of an extremely feeble demand for the lessons of Christianity. The rapid increase of human beings is followed up, at a very sluggish and unequal pace, by an increase in the means of religious instruction. The effect of this lethargy is, that whole breadths of territory are in a state of spiritual desolation; and the families by whom they are occupied, almost utter strangers to the habits or the decencies of a Christian land, are represented as being scarcely above a state of practical heathenism.*

3. But instead of drawing our argument from the uncertainties of a dim and distant region—we may only look nearer home, to have the very same exhibition of our nature immediately under our eyes. It is true that we have an endowed church; which was formerly more adequate than it is now to the wants of our population. But many are the towns and parishes of our land where

---

* See Note I, Appendix.

the population has vastly outgrown the means of Christian instruction within the pale of the establishment—and it is interesting to mark in how far the deficiency has been made up by the spontaneous efforts of those who are unable to find admittance into its churches. It is unquestionable, that dissenters have done much by their chapels to supplement the deficiency; but it were an utter mistake to imagine that they have nearly overtaken it. The truth is, that, in our large cities, and more especially in their suburbs, as well as in those manufacturing districts which so teem with recent villages, and whose every establishment has its cluster of families—it may with all safety be affirmed, that greatly more than one half of the people of sufficient age for church-going attend nowhere; and that they neither own nor occupy seats in any place of worship whatever. The sectarians, with all their activity and zeal, notwithstanding the fullest toleration for their efforts, have not been able to pervade this impenetrable mass—and the profaneness and profligacy of the multitude just deepen and accumulate the more with every augmentation of their numbers. It is quite palpable that the people do not seek after the article of Christian instruction as they would after an article of ordinary merchandise. This appears most patently in all those cases where the people have multiplied beyond the establishment— and we may infer the melancholy result, if without an establishment altogether, they had been left to no other principle than that of demand and supply over the whole length and breadth of the land.

4. This, then, is the good of an establishment. The people, instead of being left to go in quest of religious instruction, have, by its means, the instruction obtruded upon them. Generally speaking, they have not so much of desire or demand for the article, as that they shall themselves originate the movement towards it, and far less travel the whole distance, and make all the efforts and all the sacrifices necessary to obtain it. In the vast majority of instances, would neither the requisite trouble be taken, nor the requisite expense be incurred. They have not enough of native appetite to create an effective demand for the food; and, unlike to the corporeal, the want of this food, instead of whetting the spiritual appetite, would only dull and deaden it the more. We have therefore no doubt, that, on the event of our establishment being swept away, and a mere system of free trade being substituted in its place, the moral effect would be tremendous. That which gave activity and healthful impulse to the commerce of our land, would be of withering effect upon its Christianity. Let the machinery, if needful, be actuated by the force and the fire of another principle —let all its rust and other unhingements be done away—let it be provided with more efficient workmen—and every thing be done so as that it shall

H

perform its evolutions more sweetly and yet more powerfully than before—but let it not be taken down. It never will be replaced by the sponta. neous act, or kept in operation by the spontaneous habit of the people. It may be better wrought at one time, and worse at another; but, even with all its corruptions, our establishment is a stay and a safe-guard—and a helpless, a headlong degeneracy would ensue from the demolition of it.

5. And an establishment might be so framed, as, by a sufficient multiplication of parishes, to pervade the whole mass of society. Let each family be provided with a church so near, that by an easy Sabbath-day's journey they might enjoy the stated ministrations of a clergyman, and each clergyman be provided with a territory so moderate and manageable, that, by his week-day movements, he can ply the attentions of Christianity and kindness with frequent reiteration upon all the families,—this were to secure, over the whole length and breadth of the land, such a juxtaposition between the gospel and every human creature, as never will be accomplished in any other way. Let such an apparatus be *well wrought;** and in no other way will a population be so thoroughly seasoned with religious instruction or so regularly served. Without this, we fear, that in every country there must be

---

* The consideration of this necessary condition is deferred to the next chapter.

unbroken fastnesses, within which men would persist always in the undisturbed heathenism of nature; and whence they would never, by any primary will of their own, go forth to the lessons, or emerge into the light of Christianity. They must be assailed from without—and that, not by transient or migratory invaders, but such as shall, having made good their lodgment, keep perpetual occupancy within the borders. How is it that dissenters, with all their activity, and all the freedom which they enjoy, both of effort and locomotion, have not been able to overtake this? Both in the excess of the larger country parishes, and in the growing surplus of town populations, there is ample range over which they might expatiate at pleasure. And yet the vast majority of these outfield families remain like sheep without a shepherd—aliens from the habits and the decencies of a Christian land—and demonstrate of how little avail for reclaiming them, are a mere gratuitous zeal in behalf of Christianity upon the one side, and a spontaneous demand for the lessons of Christianity upon the other. It appears but a distant expectation, that, out of these two elements alone, we shall arrive at the result of a humanized peasantry; and we should, at the least, not be so far short of it, were these outcasts provided with a sufficient number of officiating churchmen—not working gratuitously, but conscientiously alive to the duties of their station—and not waiting a spontaneous demand among the families of their allotted vineyards, but fostering that demand by the assiduity both of their pulpit and their household services.

6. We most readily admit, that ere the machine of an establishment do its full good in a country, it must be provided with men who shall work it well. It is not such a machine as supersedes the zeal and activity of Christian labourers; but it is such a machine as, when put into their hands, makes that zeal and activity ten-fold more effective. It is no argument for setting it aside, that without the devotedness of human hearts, and the diligence of human hands, it is useless. Enough, that through its intervention, any given amount of such devotedness, and such diligence, is made far more useful. It surely does not nullify the military art, that, for its best devised system of tactics, the courage of human beings is indispensable. And the same holds of spiritual tactics—one system of which may be greatly more efficient than another, although neither should be of any avail, without labour and integrity on the part of clergymen. We hold, that, by means of an endowed church, and a territorial division of the country into parishes, there is secured a greatly fuller and wider dispensation of the lessons of the gospel through the land, than by means of any such arrangement as might come spontaneously forth of all the zeal that exists for the diffusion of Christianity, on the

one hand, and of all the desire that exists for the reception of Christianity, on the other. That this zeal should have its ebbs and its alternations, is no better argument for the destruction of our establishment, than is the fluctuating supply, by inundation of water from the Nile, for effacing or filling up those ducts of conveyance which serve for the irrigation of Egypt. Though it is the descent of living water from the upper sanctuary, which transforms the sons of nature into holy and heaven-born men—this does not supersede an earthly tactics, and an earthly mechanism, for the right distribution of it. Should the Nile cease from its overflows, there would no fertilizing influence be conveyed over the land, through the dry and deserted channels by which it was intersected. And should the Spirit of God withdraw the showers of his grace from our nation, we have no such blind confidence in the virtue of frame-works, as to look for a sanctifying influence from the mechanism of pulpits and parishes. Nevertheless, it is good to uphold the sluices, and reservoirs, and aqueducts of Egypt; for when the Nile shall again rise above its banks, that is the apparatus by which its water shall be most beneficially dispersed over the fields of the territory. And nevertheless, it is good to uphold the churches, and the parsonages, and the livings of our establishment; for when the celestial influence shall again come down upon us, that is the terrestrial apparatus for the most beneficial dispersion of it among the families of our population.

7. We associate, in fancy, more of locomotion, more of itinerancy, with dissenterism; yet, in fact, an establishment, when rightly viewed, has greatly more in it of the character and power of a missionary operation. It may be regarded as a universal home-mission. It works aggressively all over the land. That was a prodigious aggressive movement which it made at the outset, when it first planted its churches, and chalked out its parishes, and so caused the voice of the gospel to be heard throughout the whole length and breadth of the territory. And then, if rightly followed up, we shall discern in its internal workings, the same character; for each minister, in his own little vineyard, is provided with ample scope, and is placed on the best vantage-ground for the high and holy functions of a Christian missionary. It is true, that his pulpit is stationary, and there must be some predisposition for Christianity among those families of his people who are drawn to it, by a process of attraction on the Sabbath. But his person is moveable; and, by a process of aggression through the week, he can go forth among all the families of his people, even among those who have as little of predisposition for Christianity, as exists in the remotest wilds of Paganism. We have not to traverse oceans and continents, in order to perform the essential work of a mission-

ary; or to assail an immortal spirit which is not in quest of salvation for itself, with the calls and overtures of heaven's high embassy. There is a moral as well as a physical distance which must be overcome; and, in the act of doing it, the parochial clergyman may have to face such difficulties, and to force his way through such barriers of dislike, or prejudice, or delicacy, that, in the prosecution of his calling, he may, without half a mile of locomotion, earn the proudest triumphs, and discharge the most arduous functions; and, in short, evince all the sound characteristics of a most deep and devoted missionary. It is true, that the same spirit may alike actuate our dissenters and our churchmen; and we must not overlook the great Christian good achieved by the former, whether in those rare and transient visitations by which they intersect our land, or in that multitude of fabrics where they permanently emanate the lessons of the gospel, and by which they have beautified, with frequent spots of surpassing verdure, the face of our island. This says much for them; but it says nothing against the effectiveness and the power which we ascribe to the machinery of an establishment, or against its fitness both for thoroughly pervading a land with the influences of Christianity, and for perpetuating these influences from generation to generation. It is most honourable to our sectarian ministers, that, unaided by the resources or facilities of an establishment, they have achieved so much ; but this does not preclude the assertion, that, with the same zeal and activity, and Christian uprightness, they could, in the capacity of churchmen, more especially of parochial clergymen, have achieved a great deal more.*

8. There is a charm in the week-day services of a parish minister, which has not been duly estimated either by philanthropists or patriots. He, in the first instance, meets with general, and I had almost said, universal welcome from the families—at least from those in the humbler classes of society. His official and recognised character furnishes him with a ready passport to every habitation ; and he will soon find, that a visit to the house of a parishioner, is the surest way of finding an access to his heart. Even the hardiest and most hopeless in vice cannot altogether withstand this influence ; and at times, in their own domestic history, there are opportunities whether by sickness, or disaster, or death, which afford a mighty advantage to the Christian kindness that is brought to bear upon them. It is thus that nature and providence may be said to act as the handmaids of Christianity, by the frequent openings which they afford to its officiating ministers ; and of which, if he do avail himself, he is sure to obtain a vast moral ascendancy over the people. Even his courtesies on the way-side are not thrown away upon

---

* See Note K, Appendix.

them ; and little do they know of humanity, who would undervalue the most passing smiles and salutations which reciprocate between a clergyman and his people, whether as the symptoms or as the efficients of a cordiality the best fitted to soften the asperities of our nature, and so to cement and harmonize the jarring elements of a commonwealth. And his week-day attentions, and their Sabbath attendance, go hand in hand. A house-going minister wins for himself a church-going people. The bland and benignant influences of his friendly converse, of his private and particular affection, are enlisted on the side of their piety—nor can we imagine a position of greater effectiveness than his, whence to bear on the hearts and habits of a surrounding population.

9. It is no personal disparagement to the dissenting minister, when we simply say of him that he is less favourably placed. He may officiate through the week among his own hearers, who often lie scattered in isolated families over a wide extent of country, or through all the streets, and to the distant outskirts of a populous town. We have no doubt that he would greatly augment his influence, by assuming a local district in either of these two situations, and, in the way of Christian experiment, charging himself with the duty of religious attention to all the families within its limits whom he shall find willing to receive him. We should look for a far wider and more welcome

respondency, and therefore a better result than is generally anticipated. But, in point of fact, this is seldom if ever done by dissenters. They are incredulous of its success—and are even themselves discouraged by a certain haunting sense of inferiority, which in as far as it is well founded, is itself a strong demonstration in favour of a religious establishment. They do apprehend a certain defect of reception and recognition among the families; and that, on the ground too, that they are not the regular or established functionaries of the land. They hang back under a sort of consciousness that theirs is not so valid a right of entry as that of the parish minister. They cannot help the feeling of a certain defect in their warrant, in virtue of which they are not so authorized to go into every house, and there overture the services of Christianity. They themselves, in short, would have a greater sense of comfort and confidence in the prosecution of such a round, if translated into the place of regular clergymen, or similarly backed by the institutions of the land. For ourselves, we should like if our dissenting ministers could in the spirit of enlightened zeal, or of active religious philanthropy, overleap all these delicacies, and actually make the attempt of carrying their household ministrations into the bosom of every family that would open the door to them. The fact that this is so little done by them, is pregnant with inference. To our mind,

it speaks powerfully for a religious establishment;
that under the cover of its sanctions, there is on
the one side, a greater boldness of access felt by
its ministers; and, on the other side, a readier acquiescence by the people, in their offered services.
The propriety of a universal movement among
the houses of his allotted territory on any Christian errand, or with any Christian proposal, is far
more promptly recognized by all, when performed
by the parish clergyman, than would be a similar
movement, if gratuitously attempted by a sectarian minister. And this would be the feeling not
of the upper classes of society alone—but, in truth,
the feeling even of workmen and cottagers. It is
one of those aptitudes of our nature, of which it
were most legitimate to avail ourselves—and which
is turned to its best account by the device of an
establishment. Without this machinery, the population will fall away in large masses, beyond the
scope of any ecclesiastical cognizance. With it a
wide door of access is opened to all the families.
It is just the access which it is most desirable that
a man of principle and prayer should be provided
with—that as it is a great, so also it may be an effectual door.*

10. The reason for such an ecclesiastical economy as we term an establishment, is founded on
certain principles which seem rooted and estab-

---

* 1 Cor. xvi. 9.

lished in the moral economy of man. One of these is a promptitude to do homage, and defer to that which is established, and just because it is so,—such a predisposition to acquiesce in the existing order of things, that we do not wait till we are satisfied of its goodness, ere the acquiescence is given, but give the acquiescence until we are provoked by its felt and ascertained badness, to resist and to disown it. The Author of our being does not trust our movements to our own slow calculations of expediency—but he inserts moving forces into our condition, which have in them the urgency of an immediate law. And it is well for the peace and settlement of a community, that the gravitation of our nature should lie so much in the direction of the powers *that be*—not so strong as to be insuperable, when these powers make outrageous violation of the rights of conscience or liberty, but yet strong enough to secure the quiescence of the aggregate society, till violence to such an amount shall have been rendered. It is a great thing for public order, that the tendencies of our nature upon this subject should, in the first instance, be sedative, and on the side of the existent authorities,—by which we mean, not the supreme only, but also the provincial and parish authorities of the land. There is a *prima facie* claim on the side of these authorities, to which there is the instant response, not of a pusillanimous, but of a proper and well-principled homage

on the part of the people. It is thus, that when
a monarch appears in the midst of his subjects,
even the most turbulent of them all cannot help
the infection, not of a slavish, but of a generous
and sentimental loyalty. It proves how conge-
nially moulded the nature of man is, to the objects of rank and office and ascendant station, that
on the moment of their presence, there is felt an
involuntary respect, of which it may almost be
said, that we lie under the moral impotency of
withholding it. It is true that the respect may be
forfeited—but this very forfeiture implies anterior
possession—and it is possession grounded on a law
of our nature, distinct from that by which we give
our esteem to virtue, or our esteem to talent, or
our esteem to personal strength, or personal loveliness. These are so many laws, but so also is
that principle by which we give our esteem to
station a law, having its own specific and substan-
tive operation in the heart of man. To be without this, would mar and deform the character,
and inflict upon it a sort of moral ungracefulness.
The man who feels disrespect for magistracy,
seems, to the general eye, as one stained with a
blemish, or disfigured by a mutilation. The man
who acts this disrespect, is, by the general voice,
chargeable with indecency.

11. These influences meet in the person of an
established clergyman—and they are greatly enhanced by the sacredness of his character. Al-

together, he stands forth so invested in the public
estimation, as to guarantee the utmost moral
security, from ought like offence being felt, or in.
sult being given, along the path of his Christian
philanthropy. His parish office will confer upon
him a fully admitted right of introduction to every
house in his parish—and, in spite of the popular
jealousy wherewith endowments are regarded, certain it is, that the popular influence of his visits,
and attentions, and labours of love, will not be
lessened, but greatly added to, if he have the
manner and independence of a gentleman. And
it saves him from a gross misinterpretation to
which he might have been otherwise exposed, that
his own personal interest is in no way dependent
on the number of his hearers. We believe that
there is a strong alliance between the household
activities of a minister, and the Sabbath attendance
of his people. But any shrewd imagination, that
so much pains were taken with the one, because
of the so much profit that accrued from the other,
would dissipate the charm and efficacy of this
operation. It is the prerogative of the established
clergyman that he is above so injurious a suspicion. He may receive payment from the state.
But in reference to the people he acts gratuitously.
There may be an indispensable routine of duties
—but all his spontaneous services bear upon them
the unequivocal aspect of pure and disinterested
zeal. And this, in the midst of a people to whom

he is every day more endeared by the kind notices and cordialities of his growing acquaintanceship, gives to all the forthgoings of an earnest parish minister, a power over the hearts and habits of families, which cannot be realized by any other individual in the commonwealth.*

12. It is a melancholy truth, that an office of such high capabilities, is, in many instances, not adequately filled. This, however, is no reason why the office should be abolished, though a most pertinent and powerful reason for its being purely and righteously patronized. The engine is not to be destroyed, because it has been sometimes wrought by incompetent or unskilful engineers. The apparatus of a church establishment is not to be taken down, because, either at present or throughout past generations, it has been under the useless or perverse management of corrupt and indolent churchmen. When the concurrence of two things is necessary to a beneficial result, we are not to demolish the one, because we have not always secured the other. The two essential conditions

---

* It is on this account, we confess, that we view the preservation of the church establishment in Ireland as a great object of national policy—being fully persuaded, that if only aright patronized, or, in other words, if wrought by zealous and efficient ministers residing in their parishes, and expatiating in all the acts of common and Christian kindness throughout their respective vicinities, it would prove the organ of a greater moral and spiritual blessing to the land, than could be achieved by any other machinery which it is possible to devise.

of usefulness, in the present instance, are a good machine, and a good mechanic; and the clear direction of wisdom is to keep up the machine, and to look out for the mechanic. The one we already have, in the frame-work of an endowed church, fitted, both by its extent and the minuteness of its subdivisions, for the conveyance of religious light and influence to every district of the land. But, for this result, it is indispensable that the working of the goodly instrument should be given to religious men. And ere the instrument should be put aside, and ere the Christianity of our people should be abandoned to the operation of those spontaneous forces, which have hitherto proved so inadequate, we should deem it greatly the better part, to uphold the establishment, and to labour in every possible way for its careful and conscientious patronage.

13. And for this inadequacy of dissenterism, we might confidently appeal to the vivid recollection of its most zealous and influential supporters; we mean its inadequacy to the object of overspreading a land with ought like a full and competent supply of religious instruction. And it is not that there is a defect in the supply of qualified ministers, but that there is a defect in that efficient demand which offers not only solicitation but support to ministers.* There are many who can both

---

* See Note L, Appendix.

feelingly and experimentally tell how strong the *vis inertiæ* is which they have oft to overcome, ere they can mature an erection for the regular performance of Sabbath services—what shifts, what entreaties, what humiliations, what heartless discouragements must all be undergone before the chapel is reared—what debts and difficulties beset the infant undertaking—and how frequently, after the house has been prepared, no such congregation can be allured, even in the midst of most populous and unprovided districts, as shall yield the barest subsistence to a minister. The country teems with these melancholy abortions; or, (should a living birth be the result of this sore labour), with the no less melancholy struggles to sustain, by all sorts of appliances, a sickly and glimmering life, that is ever on the verge of its extinction. The penurious, and sometimes the disgraceful allowance on which the minister even of affluent hearers is permitted to bring up a family in·starvation and sordidness, speaks powerfully on the side of our argument. It demonstrates the strength of that barrier, which nothing, we apprehend, but the energies of an endowed church can force and overcome. The system of meeting-houses can only be carried to a certain extent over the face of society—after which, and at its extreme margin, it can no longer summon the people to effectual co-operation, having then to encounter a sluggishness, a spiritual inertness, which it finds to be impracticable. Within this margin there may be, there are dissenting congregations which flourish in point of number, and dissenting ministers who are comfortably and respectably maintained by them. It is near to this margin when the contest begins to be tough and arduous, and at length altogether hopeless. A fraction, and but a fraction of the species may thus be brought into contact with the word and ordinances of religion. But the impotency of the expedient would be felt long before half the species were overtaken; and with no other system than that of free trade in Christianity, the vast majority of every land, would, in respect even of means and ordinances, be left in a state of practical heathenism.

14. In all ages of the church, there has been room for the complaint, as well as for the prayer founded upon it—that the harvest is plenteous, but the labourers are few. Yet, if the greater number of the fields which contain this harvest be inaccessible, there might be more labourers than can be admitted to that part of the harvest which may be approached. We, therefore, see no inconsistency between the general position, that there is a paucity of efficient ministers when compared with the population; and the actual state of the sectarians, among whom, on the one hand, "there are many ministers of irreproachable character at this time unable to obtain pastoral engagements," and, on the other hand, "there are

many stations highly interesting and important,
that are suffering greatly from the want of able
and learned ministers." We hold, that, by means
of an establishment, the great national vineyard is
thoroughly intersected, by roads to every parish,
and even by footpaths to every little hamlet and
cottage of the land. It is thus that avenues are
opened up, throughout all, even the minutest subdivisions of that territory by which the harvest is
borne; and then does the prayer obtain its most
emphatic fulfilment, when, by a blessing poured
forth from on high on the churches of the establishment, its ecclesiastics, under the visitation of a
new spirit, labour more abundantly than before,
each in his own homestead, and so leaven with
Christianity, the whole mass of that population
wherewith they are so extensively mingled.

15. But though we hold a revival in the establishment to be the likeliest mean by far for the
revival of Christianity in our land, such a conviction of the might and efficacy which belong to a
national church, does not preclude the conviction,
that it is of the very highest importance to have
an active, unrestrained, and fully tolerated dissenterism. This latter will never, we think, supersede an establishment; but it may stimulate that
establishment to a ten-fold degree of effectiveness.
It may act by a moral compulsion, not merely on
its existing clergymen, but on those holders of patronage and power to whom we have to look for

our future clergymen. For this purpose, it is well that sectarianism should flourish and prevail, even to the degree of alarming the dignitaries of our land for the safety of its ecclesiastical institutions—of reducing them to the necessity of providing these institutions with those functionaries who are best fitted, by their talent and their piety, to uphold the church in public estimation. We should therefore like, on the one hand, to behold dissenters in the full glow of activity all over the land, for out of the disturbance thus given to our high church exclusionists, we should anticipate the happiest consequences. We question not, that there is a great direct service rendered to Christianity by the instrumentality of sectarians. But we have ever reckoned it their chief service, that they set in motion, and in more efficient play, a far more powerful instrumentality than any which is wielded by themselves. They are not the best fitted for working a general religious effect upon the population. But they give impulse to that apparatus which is best fitted for it. They do not themselves form an effectual mechanism for operating throughout a whole aggregate of human beings. But they, nevertheless, occupy a high place of command, for they touch the springs of that mechanism which is effectual. It is to the intervention of the church, in fact, that they owe their greatest usefulness; for, by moving that which most powerfully moves and effects general

society, they might do more for the religion of the
people, than by the application of their own immediate hand to the hearts and consciences of individuals. With these views, sectarians on the
one hand might bless and honour the church,
while on the other hand the warmest friends of
the church might look with benignant welcome
on the zeal and prosperity of sectarians. They
have done much for Christianity by the congregations which they have formed in towns and crowded
parishes, and by the conversions which they have
achieved in families. But the benefit which they
have wrought, by their wholesome reflex influence on the Establishment, is above all computation.

16. In every great question upon which two
parties have been formed, the difficulty is, to
construct the right system, by adopting the excel-
lencies and avoiding the errors of both. The
parties themselves move in masses. They act
gregariously. And hence, in spite of all that is
said about the ascendancy of rational opinion in
this our enlightened day, there is really much of
the blind and the headlong in the operation of
those moral forces which decide the practical measures, and influence the general state of society.
Men take their direction and their impulse from
the broad aspect of things—and when once they
take their stand with either side of a controversy,
and read nothing but hate and hostility in all that

is opposed to them, they find it a far easier work than that of discrimination, simply to urge forward whatever shall make for the one side, and shall make against the other. It is thus that the bigots of an establishment are for putting down all sectarianism; and that the zealots of sectarianism are for rooting up all establishments. They regard not how beautifully it is, that these two rival interests act and re-act for the good of a population—so that the perfection of an ecclesiastical system lies in the ample endowment of the one, and the ample toleration of the other. Without an establishment, the light of religious instruction would shine forth but rarely, or be spread but superficially over a land. Without a free and active dissent, that light might wane to its extinction and become darkness—the establishment, reposing in its undisturbed security, would become inert and inefficient, or, along with the intolerance, might be further deformed by all the corruptions of Popery.

17. The sectaries act upon the establishment, as we have already said that the proposed university of London is fitted to do on those of Oxford and Cambridge; that is to say, not so as to supersede, but so as to stimulate, and thereby to uphold the character and stability of the national institutions. As it is with common, so it is with Christian education. By the establishment of parochial schools the former has become a universal blessing

among the peasantry of our Lowland parishes in Scotland. Yet how frenzied were that bigotry which should denounce those private and subscription schools, that have accommodated the families for whom there was no room in the endowed seminary, or, perhaps, even drawn away some families from their wonted attendance on the parish schoolmaster. This latter they can only in general do by the superior scholarship which they afford—and this is an advantage which they can continue to hold only until, by a pure exercise of patronage, the parish school is again provided with an able and efficient functionary. And this reasoning applies exactly to the case of a parish church. It may, for a whole incumbency, labour under an inferiority in the style of its ministrations to the adjacent meeting-house—and may give token, by its deserted pews, to the surpassing energy and zeal of the sectarian over the regular clergyman. This casts a temporary obscuration over the establishment; but not in the slightest degree to endanger its perpetuity. By a new appointment the recovery either is or may be made. And such, after all, is the native preference of the people for the establishment, that nothing but a right and conscientious patronage is required to keep the vast bulk of our families within its pale.

18. But we may here notice a very observable difference between the case of science, and that of religion—even though it is a difference which does

not affect the essential or the general argument for endowments in behalf of either. Our argument, in the former case, is, that unless pure science be thus upholden, it will vanish from our land— for it lies greatly too remote both from the popular understanding, and the popular taste, to be upholden by the spontaneous demand of society for its lessons. But it cannot be said of pure Christianity—either that it is above the popular understanding, or repugnant to the popular taste. According to our apprehensions of the gospel, the pure and the popular are mainly at one—and its most characteristic doctrines find a readier coalescence with the intellect and affections of the humbler, than with those of the higher classes of our community. That conviction in some truth of philosophy which is wrought laboriously into the mind by arduous demonstration, differs from that instant recognition which is given to some religious truth, when, by the immediate light of its own evidence, it finds its way to the consciences of men. In human learning, the people, naturally averse to mental labour, would prefer to be taught superficially rather than scientifically—and hence, if lofty and rigorous science is to be upheld in a land, there must, to compensate for the small number of students, be salaries for teachers, and even a compulsory attendance upon their instructions. But, in divine learning—*if once the people are assembled to its lessons,* their clear preference

is for the scriptural and the sound representations
of Christianity to those more meagre exhibitions
of the truth in which mere moralists or sentimen-
talists indulge. Let there be any incipient ear-
nestness about religion at all; and the doctrines of
the New Testament, in its whole depth and peculiarity, is felt to be the ministration which is best
suited to it. In science, the class-room of severe
demonstration is attended by the few, while the
class-room of showy experiment is attended by
the many. It is to retain and perpetuate the former style of instruction in a land that college
endowments are necessary. In religion, those
churches where the momentous realities of the
question are glossed over by false and flimsy representations of it is attended by the few, while
that church where the truth in all its nakedness
is most faithfully expounded, and where the most
severe and searching applications of it are made
unto the conscience, is attended by the many. It
is not then for the sake of upholding a sound
against a spurious Christianity that church endowments are necessary ; for in truth, the lessons of
the former are far more congenial with the taste of
the multitude than those of the latter. But they are
necessary for upholding Christianity, in any of its
forms, against the lethargic indifference of nature
to Christianity in all its forms. Once the multitude is addressed with Christianity, their native
preference is for the sound rather than the spuri-

ous. But still they need to be so addressed—for of themselves they will go in quest of neither. The thing to be overcome is not their resistance to the sound religion because of their love to the spurious. But the thing to be overcome, is their *vis inertiæ* in reference to religion at all. That is the point which needs to be carried—and, instrumentally speaking, it only can be carried, we apprehend, through all the corners of our land, and through all the classes of society, by the forces of an establishment. After that, by this device, the sound of *a* gospel is heard in every parish, it is a mighty auxiliary on the side of true religion, that the relish and preference of the multitude should be for the lessons of *the* gospel. The establishment has the effect, in the first instance, of carrying a general Christianity, in bulk, or in the gross, throughout a whole population. Let this establishment be well patronized—and then each zealous and efficient clergyman, in his own special vineyard, would rally around the altar at which he officiates his own separate portion of the population. It is in this way a noble machine for the thorough Christianization of a land. It is true that, without an evangelical ministry, it will not accomplish the service. But its superiority, in point of tuition, to a system of dissenterism, remains notwithstanding—for, under the latter, the service cannot be accomplished whether without an evangelical ministry, or with one.

19. But this it is which has disguised the merits of our question from the eye of the public. What we affirm is the superiority of an establishment as a *machine*, whether for Christian or for common education, to that merely natural mechanism, whose alone impellent force is the spontaneous demand of society. But this machine will not give full experimental proof of its efficacy, unless it is provided with good workmen—and so its power and properties may lie altogether hidden, because of the incompetent hands to which it has been committed. It is thus that the adversary of endowments has frequently too much colour for a triumphant appeal in the actual state of the church and universities; and he is enabled, when the one is filled with ungodly clergymen, and the other with indolent or illiterate professors, to speak with plausibility of the uselessness of both. Nevertheless, it may hold true, and most importantly true, that, in point of enginery, there is nothing nearly so effective as a system of endowments; and that though, when placed under the heavy disadvantage of being administered by men who are corrupt or careless, it does little for the land—yet that men of talent and virtue can work off a tenfold benefit, when the means and capabilities of such an apparatus are entrusted to them. When viewed as a question of national or philanthropic policy, it should not be difficult to say, whether it is better to have a system under which lofty science and a

fully diffused Christianity may be served out to the country—and without which, it seems neither possible to sustain the purity of the one, or adequately to circulate the other through the mass and interior of a country's population. The alternative is not, we admit, between a state of things in which these blessings *must* be, and a state of things in which they cannot be; but between a state of things in which they *may* be, and in which they cannot be. Even though we should be able to allege no more for our cause, this we hold to be a mighty allegation in its favour—and it does appear an unwise and a harsh conclusion, that because in the former state of things it is in the power of bad or indifferent men to render an establishment inert and inefficient, we must therefore be precipitated into the latter state of things, when, without an establishment, the power of the good and the able shall be abridged tenfold. Because a frame-work in the hands of the worthless does nothing, that surely is no reason against the erection of it, if it can be demonstrated, that, in the hands of those who are competent to its management, it is vastly more productive of good than even without such an instrumentality they are able to do for the commonwealth. That should be the system in every land which gives fullest scope to the zeal and energies of the righteous, even though it should become altogether effete in those seasons of moral degeneracy when the righteous have disappeared.

Then it is true, that an establishment becomes worthless and withered like the skeleton of dry bones in the vision of Ezekiel,—yet, rather than take down the fabric, and scatter it into fragments —better, we deem, to pray for that vivifying Spirit which comes down from on high, when "the Lord God will cause breath to enter into it, and it shall live."

CHAPTER IV.

ON THE ABUSE OF ENDOWMENTS.

1. To realize our *beau ideal* of a good educational system in the land, there must, in the first instance, be the erection of a right machine, and, in the second instance, the appointment of right men to work it. The two ingredients which must meet together for this purpose, are an adequately endowed establishment on the one hand, and a virtuous patronage on the other. There may be a wealthy establishment without a virtuous patronage, or it can be imagined, that there may be in great force throughout the land, the principle which would lead to a virtuous patronage, but withal a meagre and ill-provided establishment. In either way, we think that the interests whether of learning or religion would be greatly abridged; and that, to make out a full security for these interests, we should neither acquiesce in our possession of but the one ingredient while the other is awanting, nor far less expunge the one because the other is awanting, without which it is comparatively useless—but we should strenuously endeavour to realize the combination of both.

2. If we have succeeded in our foregoing argument, it will be evident—First, that a population

are in far unlikelier circumstances for being pervaded with Christian instruction, when left to their
own natural demand for it, instead of its being offered and obtruded upon them by means of
churches ready made to their hands, and ministers within these churches, who each, within the
moderate and manageable territory assigned to
him, shall charge himself, both in his pulpit and
throughout his parish, with the care of the religion
of the families. And, secondly, that even for the
elementary scholarship which should be acquired
by all, there is no apparatus so efficient as a
scholastic establishment at least partially endowed; and that, for a higher scholarship, there
is need of a larger endowment. If there be truth
in this principle, it points emphatically to a more
liberal endowment for the universities of Scotland.
The improvement chiefly required is to raise the
preliminary education, that so rising from this
higher commencement, we may raise all the pos-
terior education of our students, and send them
forth far more accomplished in high erudition and
philosophy, than they are under our present system. But for this purpose, the professors must
be men of loftier science than at least they need
to be at present; and the task which shall then be
put into their hands, can only be well achieved by
men of rarer and higher qualifications. Now, for
reasons which have already been abundantly insisted on, they will, after this ascent to a higher

species of literary labour, have fewer students than before—standing then at a greater distance from the popular taste, and placed more beyond the reach of the popular and general demand for education. In other words, by one and the same movement, they are called to a higher service, yet condemned to a lower recompense than before. This is not the way in which the more scarce or the more valuable is secured in any other department of human affairs; and we therefore fear that, in this department, competent labourers for the then greater mental or literary labour will not be obtained, unless some compensation be provided for the sure reduction that must take place in the attendance upon seminaries, when there shall be a more remote and recondite science, and when all the courses of instruction shall be more elaborate than before. We can perceive no way of rectifying this inconvenience, but by larger fees or larger salaries,—and as by the former expedient, a still greater reduction must be effected on the attendance, we are not aware of any sure method by which the cause of a loftier learning can be upheld in our land, but by a larger endowment coming in aid of a smaller attendance. It is thus that, for one of the purest and brightest glories of a nation, even its science and literature—we mean, that profound and vigorous science, and that attic literature which alone are worthy of the name— endowments more large and liberal, we fear, than our nation is willing to bestow, seem to be indispensable. On the subject, indeed, both of literary and ecclesiastical benefices, the public appear to be sadly misinformed—misled in part, perhaps, by the declamations of an honest but short-sighted patriotism, that looks with jealousy, not to their misapplication alone, but also to the existence of that regular and established provision, which, if abolished, would cause Christianity to decline, and all high learning to disappear.

3. And certain it is, that there has historically been too good reason for this jealousy of endowments. The cause has become unpopular, because estimated, not by the deserts of the system itself, but by the deserts of those individual functionaries who have abridged it of its efficacy. One of the cruellest effects of official corruption is, that, in the consequent reaction of society, not only have unworthy men been despoiled of their wealth, but the country has been despoiled of a beneficial economy, which required all that wealth to uphold it in full operation. In wresting it from the hand of corruptionists, it has at the same time been wrested from the public; and the public good has grievously suffered by spoliations towards which, nevertheless, the community at large looked complacently and rejoiced. This was remarkably verified at the time of the Reformation, when the church was shorn of its patrimony; and revenues which might have been assigned to the support of

Christian instruction in extensive and over-peopled parishes, were absorbed into a state of mere property by the rapacity of individuals. Thus it is too that church lands, and prior acres, and bishop rents, and lay impropriations of tithes, and many other vestiges of the opulence in this country of the establishments of former days, have merged either into personal ownership, or into the possession of the crown; and in both ways, (in the latter through the medium of pensions) they have been transferred from the object of public usefulness, to the object of upholding the splendour and opulence of private families. And the result of that which was contemplated at the time with a sort of generous satisfaction, has been the aggrandizement of individuals at the expense of the common weal; the sacrifice of great public interests, because the sacrifice of great public institutions, at the shrine of cupidity; the enrichment of the landed aristocracy, it is true, but this with sore prejudice to the best elements of a nation's greatness—the learning of its upper classes—the piety and moral worth of its general population.

4. Such has been the melancholy result of that blind and impetuous vengeance that was called forth by the vices of the Popish clergy. Society were scandalized; and they regarded, not with tolerance merely, but with high gratification, the plunder of the ecclesiastical benefices. Knox, and the other heads of the reformation, saw the

mischief, and endeavoured to avert it; and had
their representations been listened to, we should
have had both a better endowed church, and perhaps the most perfect collegiate system of any nation in Europe. Not merely might our present
universities have been upheld in full equipment,
but we should have had in our chief provincial
towns, endowed seminaries of a higher class than
parish schools. The funds that were absorbed
during the period of that unprincipled scramble,
would not only have sustained a sufficient number
of functionaries, for the purposes both of literary
and Christian education, but there would have
been enough, and to spare, for the decent and respectable maintenance of them all. What a fine
national object would have been gained, had there
been a sufficiency reserved for a seemly income
to our parochial schoolmasters; so that instead of
men sunken in poverty, and but on a level with
the peasantry by whom they are surrounded, we
should have had men who superadded the weight
of station to that of office, in contact throughout
all our parishes with the families of our general
population. This also has gone to wreck, along
with the other noble interests which perished in
the wildness of that revolutionary storm; and in
this little age of calculators and economists, there
are patriots who can rejoice in such a consumma-
tion. The age of moral chivalry is gone.

5. Still we must admit, that, even in our own

days, there is too good reason for a jealousy of endowments. We believe, that to secure a higher style of education at our universities, larger salaries would, in many instances, be indispensable. But let these once be established, and they instantly become objects for a common-place ambition. They can be imagined of such value, that, independently of fees, they might be sought and aspired after by men of family; and, whereas now they are exposed to invasion from the mere underlings of political subserviency, they might then be alike exposed, from placemen of a higher walk, whose present game is among the offices of a prouder and a wealthier preferment. It is not then by a more liberal endowment of professorships, that we escape the danger of their lapsing into sinecures. We may, in fact, aggravate the danger, and render a virtuous and vigilant patronage still more requisite than before. This is the precise difficulty which meets us in advocating the cause of endowments. We hold them to be a *sine qua non*, for the purposes either of a diffused Christianity, or of a sustained philosophy in our land ; and yet, in respect of both these purposes, they are liable to be nullified. The task we have undertaken, is to uphold the necessity of one ingredient, which, nevertheless, by the access of another ingredient, may at once be neutralized. We trust it is obvious to our readers, that this does not annihilate the importance or significancy of our argument. We have endeavoured to show, that, what in the business of ordinary trade would be stigmatized as an artificial bounty, is so indispensable in the business of education, that without it, Christian education would be greatly abridged in point of extent, and scientific education be greatly reduced beneath the eminence of that pure and high philosophy to which it should be carried. Yet there is a blight of corruption by which the whole power and promise of a system of endowments might be cruelly undone; and we proceed to offer a few considerations, on which society may now hopefully look forward to a mitigation of this evil.

6. But we would, in the first place, remark, that in reference to the great majority of our existing endowments, there is a frequent, but a most unfair method of estimating the burden of them to the commonwealth. The wealth which sustains them, is not wrung by taxation from the other orders of the state. They are a species of property—held, no doubt, by a particular tenure—but still coeval, at least, with the great mass of actual property in the land. The territorial estates of Oxford, and Cambridge, and Glasgow, and St. Andrews, and Aberdeen, are, on the whole, of higher antiquity, as possessed by these corporations, than far the greater number of landed properties in the island, as held by private individuals. The public are no more entitled to regard these university domains in the light of an usurpation,

than one squire is to look upon the acres of his neighbouring squire, as having been wrested by injurious encroachment from himself. No doubt, he would have been all the richer, had it so happened that both properties had been merged into one, and descended by inheritance to his own family; and he may look with cupidity to fields which he dare not appropriate. And it is just with a cupidity as unreasonable, that some, in the guise too of patriotism and public virtue, would eye the patrimony both of church and college, and would even look with somewhat of the same complacency as to the triumph of liberality and justice, if it were made the subject of general spoliation. Yet it remains a truth, that neither are tithes, nor church and college lands, a burden upon any man. In virtue of these, the property of our nation has come down to the present age, either more divided than it would otherwise have been, or so much of it in the possession of public functionaries, instead of being in the possession of men, who, simple proprietors, or " nati consumere fruges," have had no function assigned to them. As it is, that property is owned by men, who, in return for it, do something. Otherwise, that property would have been owned by men, who, in return for it, did nothing. This is the real state of the alternative; and when so viewed, we may fearlessly commit the question of our literary and ecclesiastical establishments to its trial. Even

had they simply been harmless, or if the harm
they have done, is barely in equipoise with the
good, it has not been worse for the country than
if these obnoxious endowments never had existed.
This is the true point from which the reasoning
should take its departure; or this the level of zero,
from which the positive argument in favour of establishments is raised. The service they have
done, may not be very calculable, and yet be very
great; for what would have been the religion of
our country without the churches of England and
Scotland; or what its science without the universities of both?

7. But this, though enough to silence the hostility of those who are the adversaries of establishments, should not be enough to satisfy their
friends. It were well, if the service rendered to
society, by churches and colleges, could be augmented ten-fold; and besides, we are pleading for
something more than the toleration of their present endowments. We plead for the extension of
them. And the question recurs, how are the requisite grants to be guarded against the abuse to
which they are so readily exposed, by the worthless nominations of a corrupt and unprincipled patronage?

8. We will not extenuate or conceal the difficulties of this question. We scarcely know a
more arduous problem in the philosophy of human
affairs, than the construction of a right board or

body of patronage. We are unable to offer an infallible specific upon this subject; and have a far stronger apprehension of the danger, than confidence in the benefits or the safety of any method that has been proposed. It is true that we look forward, and sanguinely too, to a better and a purer direction of the patronage than heretofore; but that, not because of any virtue in the constitution of a different frame-work, or of a more skilful mechanism in the construction of that body by whom the election shall be made, or in whom the power of the appointment shall be vested. We think, that under every variety of frame-work, the principle of corruption is ready to operate; and it is only because of the stronger moral counteractive to this, that we hope, under all the varieties, henceforth to behold a series of more virtuous and patriotic nominations.

9. It is no infallible preservative against corruption, that the patronage of college livings be vested in the members of Faculty, or in the Senatus Academicus. One might, *a priori*, have imagined that there could not be a better security for right nominations, than that they should be thus vested—seeing that all the professors participate, more or less, in the benefits of that larger attendance, which the distinguished merit of any one individual of their body has the effect of drawing to their seminary. But there are personal and family considerations which overbalance this. And

hence, the hereditary successions in colleges which are thus patronized—the firm and infrangible compacts which sometimes last for generations, cemented as they are by the affinities of blood and of relationship—the decaying lustre of chairs once occupied by men of highest celebrity and talent, but the very ascendancy of whose influence when living, or of whose names after they were dead, effected the transmission of their offices to a list of descendants. We should expect this corruption to be more incidental to the remote or provincial colleges—the proceedings and the policy of which are farthest removed from the glare of public observation. Yet no one can deny, that, even under this form of patronage, a visible improvement is going on—though it must be confessed, that it is perhaps, of all others, the form least compatible with the public benefit, under such an augmentation of endowments as we would recommend. The effect of that augmentation were to increase still further the proportion of the salaries to the fees, in that part of revenue which is independent of merit and exertion, to that part of it which merit and exertion alone have the tendency to enlarge. The temptation to an interested appointment thus becomes greater, while the prejudice inflicted by it on the whole income of the corporation, would be proportionally less. For these reasons, we should not object, though, contemporaneously with an addition to the professorial salaries, there was a commutation of the professorial patronage—a transference of this power to some other quarter, where it should be less exposed to the hazard of being worthlessly exercised.

10. Another method is, to vest the patronage in a body exoteric to the college, as in the corporation of the town where the university is situated. We believe, that, notwithstanding the literary disqualifications of many of the electors, the nominations under this mode of patronage in Scotland, will stand a most honourable comparison with all the others. It is remarkable, that some of the chief deviations by magistrates and councils in the exercise of this trust, have been brought about by the influence of leading men whether in the church or in the university. This certainly makes against the first mode of patronage; and it is saying much for the second, that when the patrons are left to themselves, they do feel in such considerable degree the guidance of the public voice, and are so often the willing organs for giving expression and effect to the public opinion. The force of this engine has mightily increased within these few years; and accordingly, the improvement of all city patronage, whether in the disposal of church or college livings, has become quite palpable.

11. The third mode of patronage is to vest it in the crown. The causes of corruption under this form are too obvious to be insisted on; yet who can deny the growing strength of those counter-

active forces, by which, even under this modification, there is now a far purer and wholesomer exercise of the patronage. There is an energy in the collective voice of society that was before unfelt—a call from the public to which statesmen now find it their truest policy to conform; and by the contemptuous disregard of which for years, the ascendant influence of our land has at last been wrenched from that basis on which it had been so long and so inveterately settled. Scotland now breathes a freer air than it did but months ago—and any attempt to keep down the heavings of the public mind towards a purer and more righteous system, were like the wretched impotency of Xerxes lashing the Hellespont. It were a vain endeavour to stem that torrent which sooner or later must carry all before it; and as well might corruption try, at the bidding of her voice, to seal up the winds of heaven, or to lay an arrest on the courses of the firmament.

12. We have no other remark to offer, in regard to the last mode of patronage which we shall at present notice, namely, that which is exercised by private individuals—than that, more or less, it participates in the same improvement of its character —and that, too, by the same influence. The dominant spirit of the times, in fact, runs through all the channels of the existing organization of society; and a sense of character, under the vigilant notice of the many-eyed Argus, operates with

a force that was never before known in any by-
gone period of our history. There is now a greater
value felt for public gratitude and public esteem;
and this does come powerfully in aid of a higher
principle, both with the many private patronages
of our church, and with the few of our universities. A careless and unprincipled act of patronage would be more felt now than ever by the general mind as a moral violence, and would be more
resented as such by the general voice. It is certainly more to this that we look for our prospect
of brighter days, as far as they can be realized by
a more effective official agency in all the departments both of the church and of the state, than to
any changes in the law or methods of our existing
patronage. There is a corrective and a controlling
force in the opinion of society, which now operates
with salutary effect on all these methods; and, independently of any ameliorations in the form, we
cannot but anticipate, from every thing which
passes before our eyes, a very great amelioration in
the substance and spirit of all patronage.*

13. Now, it is this which gives comfort and
confidence in pleading the cause of endowments.
Is that the time either for abridging them or for
arresting their progress, when the security for a
righteous dispensation of them is so obviously upon
the increase? Are we now to abstract or to with-

---

* See Note M, Appendix.

hold the one indispensable ingredient, when the
other ingredient, alike indispensable to a prosper-
ous result, is supplied more plentifully than before?
Even with all the jobbing and low jockeyship that
may have been concerned in the appointments of
other days, is there any prepared to affirm, that it
would have been better for the science and religion
of our land, had these interests been left to their
chance; and the country been suffered to proceed without her church, and without her universities? And if good has been done by the endowments which support these, in what, comparatively
speaking, some would be disposed to term a reign
of profligacy, what greater good may now be
anticipated, under the evident advances of a reign
of principle? Shall we demolish that apparatus
which, even with workmen fetched to it at random,
has wrought off such an incalculable amount of
benefit to society, at the very time when workmen
are beginning to be selected with greater care;
and is the best enginery for a great and beneficent
result to be set aside, just when the demand of the
public has become more effectual than ever for the
best engine-men? Now, if ever, is the time when,
side by side with the growing securities for a righteous patronage, there should be a growth of endowments towards, if not all at once to, the farthest limit of their usefulness; when, like the
ascent of an ordinate from its minimum state,
there should at least be in progress the re-ascent,

both of clergy and professors, to the status from which they have so immeasurably fallen; and when emancipated from the straits of a condition certainly too beset and limited, the dignitaries of learning should be placed in more fit and seemly relation, than that in which they have stood for half a century, to the other dignitaries of our land.*

14. There is one species of abuse on which I do not propose to enter—the mal-administration of college revenues. The Royal Commission of Inquiry now sitting on the universities of Scotland will, there is every reason to believe, place this matter on a satisfactory footing; and there is one reason connected with the interest of these endowments, which makes it strongly advisable that every thing connected either with fees, or bursaries, or salaries, should be perfectly open to public observation. It will give confidence, and along with it liberality to the authors of bequests. The Farquhars of future times will feel security, when they find that such munificence as his is not misapplied. In this view, it is of the utmost importance that our universities should no longer re-

---

* We have data for fixing the relation in which the various public functionaries, whether of the church, of the law, of the army and navy, or of colleges, stood to each other, and to the proprietors of land a century ago, in the revenues which were then attached to the respective offices, and in the rentals of estates. We have also lower, though not perhaps less satisfactory data, in the traditions of that period respecting the state of society, and more especially the intermarriages of families.

tain the character of close corporations—and that
the light of day should be admitted upon all our
doings. We have no doubt, that first, the imagination of our unbounded wealth, and, secondly,
a distrust founded on the ignorance of its application—that these two things have chilled the gener-
osity of many, who, otherwise, would have gladly
associated their names with new or more extended
endowments in behalf of education. In either
view, a system of publicity is most desirable, both
that men of wealth and patriotism should see the
nakedness of our land, and that they should have
the fullest guarantee against any abuse or perver-
sion of their bounty. When made fully acquainted
with the actual state of our colleges, they will be
at no loss for the right subjects of testamentary
beneficence, as the foundation of a bursary, with
some qualification of merit or proficiency annexed
to it—or that of a new lectureship for some science
not yet provided in the scheme of education—or
that of an ecclesiastical ministration to the students, whether in the shape of a regular Sabbath
service, or a course of week-day addresses, on some
topic connected with the evidences or the doctrines
of Christianity—or the establishment of tutorships,
by which young men of talent might be detained,
and made to act a most important auxiliary part in
the business of the professor—or lastly, the extension of such of the old endowments as are found
to be inadequate. These, not to instance further

the constitution of funds for the purchase and the upholding of apparatus, or for the erection and the upholding of such fabrics as libraries, or museums, or chapels, or observatories, form the ample and inviting objects of that enlightened philanthropy which at one time devises for the interests of science, at another for the interests of sacredness —and which never makes a higher exhibition of itself, than when viewing these as conjunct interests, it blends into one the cause of learning and the cause of piety. Every thing should be done to facilitate and encourage such a career of benevolence as this. It might at length approximate our universities to those of wealthy and well-endowed England, which, fostered as they have been into magnitude by the liberality of former ages, require only an impulse from the wholesome jealousy of the present age, to give them all that might and momentum in society, of which they are so abundantly capable.

15. But if this spirit of testamentary benevolence were once awakened, it would have a boundless variety of other objects connected with education, beside the full equipment of colleges. There still lies an immeasurable field before us in the needs of our growing population, both for common and Christian instruction. What a multiplication, for example, must there be of local or district schools, ere the plebeian orders of any of our large cities can all be overtaken. How many

even are the provincial parishes where the number
of people has outstripped three or four times over
what was found to be an adequate provision of
scholarship a century ago. What an opening to
Christian benevolence is presented in the enor-
mous magnitude of those town parishes, where so
many chapels are required to supplement the one
church, which is all that our establishment has
provided for the accommodation of many thousands! Altogether, the apparatus, the system
of means or of instrumentality in our land is
greatly short of its moral, and educational, and
religious necessities. There is room not merely
for an immense number, but for a beautiful variety
of new endowments, corresponding to the peculiar
wants of various neighbourhoods; as of sewing
schools in the midst of a cotton-mill population,
and city missions that might be brought to bear
on the crowded vicinities of the profligate and the
poor; and itinerant teachers of different sorts
for the thinly inhabited tracts of the country; and
beside the exertion of new, the extension of old
endowments by bequests, for the augmentation of
poorer livings, or for an augmentation most ur-
gently required, even that of the salaries of our
parochial schoolmasters. This is the time, when
both popular and parliamentary vigilance is more
alive than it ever has been to the abuse of all sorts
of endowments; and this, therefore, is the time
when these endowments might be multiplied, with

L

the greatest confidence that there end shall be attained.

16. The superstition of past ages has been far more prolific of endowments, than the enlightened benevolence of the present. Some of the English colleges have been founded, and many of them enriched by Popish bequests granted in return for Popish observances. We should like to see the liberality of these days restored; but, liberality placed under the direction of wisdom and sound piety. Posterity will not pray for the souls of benefactors, they will only bless and venerate their memory. This, however, is an earthly reward; and it is well, therefore, in these days of more scriptural religion, that we can quote from the Bible passages of higher and purer encouragement. "Make to yourselves friends of the mammon of unrighteousness." "He that watereth shall be watered himself." "The liberal deviseth liberal things, and by liberal things shall he stand."

APPENDIX.

———

Of the five colleges in Scotland, it may be thought that those of Edinburgh and Glasgow should be the most exempted from that soporific influence which is ascribed to endowments; the former being very slenderly endowed, and the latter, though largely endowed, yet being, at the same time, so largely attended, as that the income from fees in the most important classes, still greatly exceeds the income from salaries. It is thus conceived, that the stimulus to exertion may be kept in full activity in these crowded and conspicuous places of education, while it is found of the more provincial colleges, where the number of students is comparatively small, that they might languish into dormitories, which, like the holds of ancient monkery, might all be swept away, without loss, or rather with the benefit of a positive relief to society.

But it is not adverted to, that in many of the largest classes, in our best frequented colleges, a very great proportion of the fees is virtually a salary. These are circumstances, which, apart altogether from the merit of the professors, or the superiority of their courses, must fix the attendance of a number of students either to Edinburgh or Glasgow. For example, let us suppose that the great population of the metropolis, and its connection with all parts of the land, and the prospects of employment which it holds out to the young men of its university, that these of themselves, should, under all the varieties of excellence in the professor of Natural Philosophy, insure to him as to the very lowest state of his class, the attendance of a hundred students; then the amount of these hundred fees forms his salary. To that extent he has a secure income; and it may act as powerfully as an opiate upon his exertions, whether it is made certain to him by a fixed and regular allowance, or by a statute of apprenticeship. We are far from lamenting this as an evil, for it is the whole drift of our argument, that without either such a salary or such a statute, there could be no Natural Philosophy purely and scientifically taught any where in Scotland. But if the statutes should do as much for the professor of the metropolitan, as the salary does for the professor of the provincial college, they really are not in such circumstances of disparity as might at the outset be imagined. Both have tasted of the opiate. Both lie under a certain temptation to indolence. If the one might remit exertion because sure of so much salary, the other might remit exertion because sure of so many students. In neither situation can this evil influence be done away; and it is by an upright patronage alone that the evil can be fully counteracted. Without this, the degeneracy of colleges is unavoidable. It is not by modelling these institutions, so that professors shall be wholly dependent on their exertions, that such degeneracy can be prevented; for, if there be any truth in our argument, science will, under such a system, dwindle into popular empiricism. Professors must to a certain, nay to a very considerable degree, be independent of the public taste, and the public demand. They are made so in the smaller colleges by salaries. And they are no less made so in the larger colleges by statutes of apprenticeship; for they are these statutes which, in all the severer parts of education, replenish our university classes. Without such independence, there must ensue the corruption of science, while, with such independence, there might ensue the indolence and unconcern of its teachers. It lays a grave responsibility upon patrons, that, in the impotency of all other expedients, there seems no method of escape from the evils, but in the righteous exercise of their trust—in the appointment of conscientious and zealous, as well as able teachers—men, at once of lofty professional acquirements, and of lofty professional enthusiasm.

Let the metropolitan professor be sure, in all circumstances, of a hundred students, and the provincial only of ten. By talent and exertion, the former may draw from his well-peopled neighbourhood and remote places together, an additional twenty. The same talent and the same exertion, might enable the latter to draw only an additional five; some of which, perhaps, may have been lured by his reputation from the other colleges. It is utterly a mistake, to imagine that this competition is too paltry to be felt. It is a competition in which the greatness of the victory is to be estimated, not by the number, but by the quality of the students; and they are only the students of a strong and decided academic taste, who, at the expense of derangement and inconvenience, will, in their preference for a better and a higher style of science, make such movements from one university to another. The homage of their selection is far more delicious to a pure collegian, than the bustling attendance, and the clamorous applauses of a crowd. It is like the praise of Atticus, the incense of which, though not copious, is exquisite, that precious aroma which fills not the general atmosphere, but by which the few and the finer spirits of our race are satisfied. Theirs is not the broad day-light of popularity. It is a fame of a higher order, upheld by the testimony of the amateurs or the *elite* in science, and grounded on those rare achievements, which the public at large can neither comprehend nor sympathize with. " They sit on a hill apart;" and there breathe of an ethereal element, in the calm brightness of an upper region, rather than in that glare and gorgeousness by which the eye of the multitude is dazzled. It is not the eclat of a bon-fire for the regaling of a mob, but the enduring though quiet lustre of a star. The place which they occupy is aloft in the galaxy of a nation's literature, where the eyes only of the more finely intellectual gaze upon them with delight, and the hearts only of such are lifted up in reverence and *con amore* towards them. Theirs is a high though hidden praise, flowing in secret course, through the *savans* of a community, and felt by every true academic to be his most appropriate reward.

Were it for nothing else than to keep this competition agoing, it were well to keep up our provincial colleges, even though they should require larger salaries for the mainten-ance of professors, while the others could be upholden on fees alone, by means of the statutes of apprenticeship. It were deciding on a hasty and superficial view, that because education was furnished to two thousand students in Edin-burgh, for less expense in salaries than to two hundred stu-dents in St. Andrews, the university of the latter place might therefore be deemed an excrescence, and dealt with accord-ingly; that is, might, with all safety and even advantage, be blotted out from the reformed scheme of colleges for Scot-land. We believe, that some imagination of this sort is very much fostered by the spectacle of only two universities in England; whereas, in our own land, there are no less than four such seats of learning. It is forgotten, that, both in Oxford and Cambridge, there is a busy competition, not merely of the one university with the other, but a strenuous internal competition amongst the numerous distinct colleges of which each university is composed. For the twenty-four seminaries of Oxford, and the sixteen of Cambridge, we have only five colleges of literature and philosophy in Scot-land; and to suppress but one of these, would be to abridge a benefit of which, in spite of the contrary appearance, we have a far less share than in the sister kingdom. To lope away any of the provincial colleges, because the professors here, secure in the possession of salaries, are in less likely circumstances for exertion, would still be to leave the metro-politan colleges secure in the possession of students, who, then limited in their choice, and bound to so many classes by a law of compulsory attendance, would make certain a larger income to the professors there than before, and cause them to be less dependent on their exertions than before. The mischief would not be annihilated. It would only be transferred; and by a process, too, which tended to augment and to confirm it. To extinguish the lesser colleges, and so put an end to their awakening rivalship, might have the effect of turning the others into two large dormitories of literature. There is a peculiarity, as we have laboured all along to demonstrate, in the higher scholarship; in virtue of which, it can less afford to have a single influence that is fitted to uphold it. We have seen, that the spontaneous demand of the public is not sufficient to uphold it; and to help out the inadequate maintenance of the professor from fees, there must be salaries. Or if, to remove this temptation to professorial indolence, the salaries are taken away, then, what would constitute another temptation equally strong, there must be statutes of apprenticeship. Such are the inherent difficulties of the case; and we should gladly avail ourselves of any other influence by which to make head against them. The competition between colleges is precisely such an influence, which, operating in some degree on the love of emolument, but in a far higher on the love of character and fame, might enlist on the side of learning and its interests, one of the most generous, and sometimes one of the strongest propensities of our nature.

There can be no doubt that it would serve to multiply and diffuse the higher scholarship through England—were the colleges of Oxford and Cambridge more dispersed than they are over the face of the country. The distance of these great seminaries, or rather of these mighty aggregates of seminaries, is a barrier in the way of many families. Let these aggregates be, in some degree at least, broken up—by detaching so many of the separate institutions, and transferring them, with all their endowments, to other parts of the land; and we feel quite confident that the whole amount of the nation's literature would be greatly increased. Each vicinity so blessed, would brighten into a more highly lettered region than before—and we should there behold a more refined and accomplished society. The juxtaposition of a college would tell on the general habit of education in every town or neighbourhood where it should happen to be situated. Such indeed is the virtue which we ascribe to salaries and statutary privileges, that should even the metropolis be made the scene of such an experiment, we fear, its unendowed university might sink under a rivalry so formidable. At all events, whatever improvements may be deemed expedient for England—we are thoroughly persuaded that the existing local distribution of colleges in Scotland should be left undisturbed—and more especially that the suppression of the provincial colleges, or the incorporation of them into one or two central universities, would both lessen the amount and enfeeble the quality of our academic education.

And indeed, under a system of incorrupt patronage, we should hold the provincial to be a likelier asylum for lofty, vigorous, and uncompromising science, than the metropolitan university. Certain it is, that professors in the latter, are under greater temptation to vitiate and debase their courses of instruction by unworthy accommodation to the taste of the city multitude. They are sure, at all events, of a large attendance from those who study for a professional object— but, over and above this, they are in circumstances for making larger additions to their attendance, by the ministration of that which shall be found most pleasing and palatable to the community around them. The danger is, lest the tone and texture of philosophy should be weakened by a commutation of the profound into the popular, by gaudy sentimentalism in the moral, or the glare of exhibition and experiment in the physical sciences. It is very well that education, even in this style, should be plentifully served out to those of the lower intellectual grades of society. But it is not well that our universities should be corrupted by it— that any departure or descent from a high academic standard should be admitted there. There is an imposing aspect of prosperity in the throng, and bustle, and excitement, of an over-crowded class-room. But it is a miserable thing —if obtained by a degrading empiricism on the part of him who conducts it. The remote professor, who sustains the dignity of his theme, even though with but ten kindred spirits to follow him on his high track of demonstration, sheds a finer lustre, and eventually confers a more substantial benefit upon the nation.

There is a grossly arithmetical style of computation on this subject; and by which a nation's best and highest interests are inconceivably brought down, by the way in which a debasing reference is made of them to a pecuniary standard. Grant that a professor, for his salary of a few hundred pounds, does no more than educate soundly every year ten or a dozen naturalists, or economists, or youthful *savants* of any description, who, by his means, shall have become thoroughly versant in one or other of the sciences—and he makes to society an adequate return in value for all that he receives. And the value is greatly enhanced, if, in addition to the produce of his own class, he shall, by his example and his efforts, give a quickening impulse to the other classes of other and rival colleges. It is true that he may not individually be an effective professor, who can either acquit himself well of his own special task, or stimulate others to the vigorous performance of theirs. This, however, is due not to the endowment, but to the wrong exercise of the patronage. The first would have wrought its effect had it not been nullified by the second. The first is that without which the public benefit cannot be achieved—the second is that without the right exercise of which the benefit will not be achieved. In all wisdom and sound policy, if we want to uphold the learning of our land, the way is, not to sweep off the first, seeing that it is indispensable—but to attend well to the second, seeing that this is also indispensable. Because the patronage has in many instances been carelessly or corruptly exercised, this is no adequate reason for destroying or even for deteriorating the endowments: The patent way is to maintain, or even extend the one, and to give, in all time coming, a purer and better direction to the other. It were hard to visit on posterity the errors of former generations; and because the men of power in the times that are gone by, have corrupted the one ingredient of a most salutary result, that we should proceed to cancel the other ingredient, and so as that the result, however salutary, or however desirable, shall be beyond the reach of any reformation.

And it is well to remark of the provincial colleges in Scotland, that the expense of their maintenance, in the great bulk of it, is not more rightfully a topic of complaint or clamour to the nation, than the expense of the maintenance or establishment of any landed gentleman. The former have a property in land or in titles, just as the latter has the ownership of an estate. The only difference between these two cases is, that the public functionaries do something—though perhaps, not all that they ought to do—but still retaining the balance in their favour; for the private gentleman, the " natus consumere fruges," does nothing. The one is pledged to a service in return for his livelihood, and some service is actually rendered. The other is pledged to no service—and the public are gainers therefore by such a distribution of the land, as that so much of it shall be allocated to the support of men, who make at least a certain return of labour for these rents, which, under another distribution, would have been absorbed by men on whom no obligation of any sort of labour was laid. It is marvellous, that with this as the real state of the case, between professors on the one hand, and proprietors on the other, one might complain of the former as being an oppressive burden upon society, and be hailed for the sentiment as a sound and enlightened patriot, and yet could not utter the same invective against the latter, without exposing himself to the charge of being an outrageous radical. There is, by the public feeling, a firmer intrenchment around the rights of the simple and absolute possessor, than around the rights of the public functionary, or any corporation of functionaries. We have no doubt that this admits of satisfactory analysis;

and we hold nothing more evident, than that a corrupt
patronage has been one great aggravating cause of the difference in question. Had clergy all been men of conscience—
or had professors all been men of learning and labour, the
rights of both would have been greatly more respected—nor
would the public have looked with so much toleration or
even complacency to those inroads on the property of either,
which, when suffered by a private individual, are denounced
and execrated as so many acts of spoliation.

Still it must be admitted, that the patrimony of the provincial colleges in Scotland, is greatly too small for the adequate endowment of them; and that to make them as respectable and efficient as they ought to be, something more
is necessary than that this patrimony should be held inviolate. There can be no doubt that the professors have
greatly declined from that status which they wont to occupy;
and that, entrusted as they are with the charge of the country's highest education, they should be preferred to a greatly
higher place in the society of our land. There is much that
is offensive to good taste, as well as to good policy, in the
want of keeping which obtains between the penury of their
condition, and the exalted nature of those functions which
they are called upon to exercise. This incongruity will be
all the more aggravated, if effectual measures are taken to
raise the standard of college education. The number of
students will be thereby lessened—and that change, which
for the upholding of our nation's literature is so imperiously
required, will at once translate our academic men into a higher
work, but into lower wages. This might be compensated
in the larger colleges by an addition to the fees—but in the
smaller colleges, there seems no other way of it, than by an
addition to the salaries. For a few thousands a year, however, we think that all the deficiencies of our university
system might be repaired. To this extent professors, instead
of independent proprietors, must become pensioners on the
public bounty. This change seems indispensable for giving effect to other and most beneficial changes, under which the mas-

ters of colleges, charged with a higher philosophy than before, may requite their more adequate maintenance, by their more arduous services.

But something more is necessary for the provincial colleges of Scotland, than a higher endowment of their existing chairs. A few more chairs would need to be instituted in order to complete them as schools of general education. In St. Andrews, more especially, the attempt should not be entertained for a moment of even so much as an approximation to a medical or a law school. But, on the other hand, we cannot imagine a fitter situation for schools of theology and general literature, both from the retirement of the place, and the facilities which it affords of moral discipline and inspection. When the young gentlemen of our higher families attend universities, it is not for any professional object, but for the general object of mental culture, and that they may go forth upon the world stored with manly and liberal acquisitions. To parents in that class of society, the very defect of law and medicine from our system should prove its recommendation; inasmuch as it secures for their sons a more select companionship. But that also is the reason why we should stand complete as a seminary of general knowledge; nor should any one branch of education be wanting to our scheme which enters into the academic education of a finished gentleman. With two or three additional classes, we could be put into an equal state of equipment for letters and philosophy with any of our sister universities; and it is to be hoped that we shall not be so overshaded by the magnitude of these, as to make our wants and our wishes be held as things of insignificance. Theirs is a magnitude made up, in great part, by the superinducement of the legal and the medical upon general scholarship: for as to the latter, we, in respect of attendance, are not many years behind the most flourishing colleges of our land. Our number of students, two years ago, was very little short from that of the general or gown students of Glasgow, at the beginning of this century: so that, instead of the suppression of the

smaller universities, or the absorption of them into the larger,
they should be upheld in their separate existence, whether
as rivals or auxiliaries—and even be put into a state of
greater sufficiency, in order to meet the growing exigencies
of our growing population.

NOTES.

Note A. page 12.

The following are among the most remarkable of those
passages in which the Author of the " Wealth of Nations"
makes known his hostility to establishments :—

" Have these public endowments contributed in general
to promote the end of their institution?   Have they contributed to encourage the diligence, and to improve the abilities
of the teachers?   Have they directed the course of education towards objects more useful, both to the individual and to
the public, than those to which it would naturally have gone
of its own accord?   It should not seem very difficult to give
at least a probable answer to each of these questions."—

" The endowments of schools and colleges have necessarily diminished, more or less, the necessity of application in
the teachers. Their subsistence, so far as it arises from their
salaries, is evidently derived from a fund altogether independent of their success and reputation in their particular professions."—

" Whatever forces a certain number of students to any
college or university, independent of the merit or reputation
of the teachers, tends more or less to diminish the necessity
of that merit or reputation."—

" The privileges of graduates in arts, in law, physic, and

divinity, when they can be obtained only by residing a certain number of years in certain universities, necessarily force a certain number of students to such universities, independent of the merit or reputation of the teachers. The privileges of graduates are a sort of statutes of apprenticeship, which have contributed to the improvement of education, just as the other statutes of apprenticeship have to that of arts and manufactures."—

" Were there no public institutions for education, no system, no science would be taught, for which there was not some demand, or which the circumstances of the time did not render it either necessary, or convenient, or at least fashionable to learn. A private teacher could never find his account in teaching either an exploded and antiquated system of a science acknowledged to be useful, or a science universally believed to be a mere useless and pedantic heap of sophistry and nonsense. Such systems, such sciences can subsist nowhere but in those incorporated societies for education, whose prosperity and revenue are in a great measure independent of their reputation, and altogether independent of their industry. Were there no public institutions for education, a gentleman, after going through, with application and abilities, the most complete course of education which the circumstances of the times were supposed to afford, could not come into the world completely ignorant of every thing which is the common subject of conversation among gentlemen and men of the world."—*Smith's Wealth of Nations*, Book V. Chapter I. Part 3. Art. 2.

Note B. page 30.

It is but justice to Dr. Smith to notice, that he admits the advantage of a school establishment for the common people, as may be seen in the following passage:—

" The education of the common people requires, perhaps,

in a civilized and commercial society, the attention of the public, more than that of people of some rank and fortune."
—" They have little time to spare for education. Their parents can scarce afford to maintain them, even in infancy. As soon as they are able to work, they must apply to some trade, by which they can earn their subsistence. That trade, too, is generally so simple and uniform, as to give little exercise to the understanding; while, at the same time, their labour is both so constant and so severe, that it leaves them little leisure and less inclination to apply to, or even to think of any thing else.

" But though the common people cannot, in any civilized society, be so well instructed as people of some rank and fortune, the most essential parts of education, however, to read, write, and account, can be acquired at so early a period of life, that the greater part, even of those who are to be bred to the lowest occupations, have time to acquire them before they can be employed in those occupations. For a very small expense, the public can facilitate, can encourage, and can even impose upon almost the whole body of the people, the necessity of acquiring these most essential parts of education.

" The public can facilitate this acquisition, by establishing in every parish or district a little school, where children may be taught for a reward so moderate, that even a common labourer may afford it: the master being partly, but not wholly paid by the public; because, if he was wholly, or even principally paid by it, he would soon learn to neglect his business. In Scotland, the establishment of such parish schools has taught almost the whole common people to read, and a very great proportion of them to write and account. In England, the establishment of charity schools has had an effect of the same kind, though not so universally, because the establishment is not so universal," &c.

This concession in favour of endowed parish schools, is made by Dr. Smith, at the expense of the dereliction of his own favourite principle. But he says what is palpably true, when he affirms that, by means of such an establishment, that elementary education which is desirable for the common people, is diffused among them far more extensively than it otherwise would be. And it appears to us just as palpable, that the establishment of endowed seminaries of a higher order, has diffused the education which is desirable both for private gentlemen, and public functionaries, far more extensively than it otherwise would be among the upper classes of society.

Note C. page 52.

The following passages from Dr. Smith speak strongly in favour of such an endowment of colleges, as might not only draw to the vacant professorships men of first-rate talents, but as might serve to detain them there in a situation confessedly the most favourable to the formation of first-rate treatises on the subjects of their respective courses:—

" In countries where church benefices are, the greater part of them, very moderate, a chair in an university is generally a better establishment than a church benefice. The universities have, in this case, the picking and choosing of their members from all the churchmen of the country, who, in every country, constitute by far the most numerous class of men of letters. Where church benefices, on the contrary, are many of them very considerable, the church naturally draws from the universities the greater part of their eminent men of letters, who generally find some patron, who does himself honour by procuring them church preferment. In the former situation, we are likely to find the universities filled with the most eminent men of letters that are to be found in the country. In the latter, we are likely to find few eminent men among them, and those few among the youngest members of the society, who are likely to be drained away from it before they can have acquired experience and knowledge enough to be of much use to it. It is observed by M. De Voltaire, that Father Porrée, a Jesuit, of no great eminence in the republic of letters, was the only professor they had ever had in France whose works were worth the reading. In a country which has produced so many eminent men of letters, it must appear somewhat singular, that scarce one of them should have been a professor in an university. The famous Cassendi was, in the beginning of his life, a professor in the university of Aix. Upon the first dawning of his genius, it was represented to him, that, by going into the church, he could easily find a much more quiet and comfortable subsistence, as well as a better situation for pursuing his studies; and he immediately followed the advice. The observation of M. De Voltaire may be applied, I believe, not only to France, but to all other Roman Catholic countries. We very rarely find in any of them an eminent man of letters, who is a professor in an university, except, perhaps, in the professions of law and physic; professions from which the church is not so likely to draw them. After the church of Rome, that of England is by far the richest and best endowed church in Christendom. In England, accordingly, the church is continually draining the universities of all their best and ablest members; and an old college tutor, who is known and distinguished in Europe as an eminent man of letters, is as rarely to be found there, as in any Roman Catholic country. In Geneva, on the contrary, in the Protestant cantons of Switzerland, in the Protestant countries of Germany, in Holland, in Scotland, in Sweden, and Denmark, the most eminent men of letters whom these countries have produced, have, not all, indeed, but the far greater part of them, been professors in universities. In these countries, the universities are continually draining the church of its most eminent men of letters.

" It may, perhaps, be worth while to remark, that, if we except the poets, a few orators, and a few historians, the far greater part of the other eminent men of letters, both of Greece and Rome, appear to have been either public or private teachers; generally either of philosophy or of rhetoric.

M

This remark will be found to hold true, from the days of Lysias and Isocrates, of Plato and Aristotle, down to those of Plutarch and Epictetus, of Suetonius and Quinctilian. To impose upon any man the necessity of teaching, year after year, in any particular branch of science, seems, in reality, to be the most effectual method for rendering him completely master of it himself. By being obliged to go every year over the same ground, if he is good for any thing, he necessarily becomes in a few years well acquainted with every part of it; and if, upon any particular point, he should form too hasty an opinion one year, when he comes, in the course of his lectures, to re-consider the same subject the year thereafter, he is very likely to correct it. As to be a teacher of sciences is certainly the natural employment of a mere man of letters, so is it likewise, perhaps, the education which is most likely to render him a man of solid learning and knowledge. The mediocrity of church benefices naturally tends to draw the greater part of men of letters in the country where it takes place, to the employment in which they can be the most useful to the public, and, at the same time, to give them the best education, perhaps, they are capable of receiving. It tends to render their learning both as solid as possible, and as useful as possible."

The attentive reader will perceive, that Dr. Smith makes the charm which works all these benefits to literature, to lie in the mediocrity of the church benefices; whereas, it lies in the superiority to those of the college benefices. It is not the deficiency of endowment in the one, but the fulness, or, at least, the excess of endowment in the other, which is the efficient cause of the good rendered to society.

NOTE D. page 58.

For the earlier history of the two English universities, the reader would do well to consult Anthony Wood's " Athenæ

Oxonienses," and Fuller's " History of the University of Cambridge." Wood's work is a history of all the writers and bish-
ops who have had their education in the university of Oxford,
from 1500 to 1695. He is, besides, the author of " Historia
et Antiquitates Universitatis Oxoniensis." The facetious
Fuller carried down his history to the middle of the seven-
teenth century. It abounds in delectable specimens of the
academic wit and humour of his day. In this work, indeed,
as well as in his " Church History of Britain," there is the
strangest mixture of amusement and information.

The moving cause of many of these endowments was superstition, as will be seen in a subsequent note. But to this
there were also many honourable exceptions. In the deed
of endowment of Clare Hall in Cambridge, the munificent
Lady De Clare professes to be actuated by " a desire for
the extension of every branch of useful learning, that there
might no longer remain an excuse for ignorance; and to
create a firmer concord and closer union among mankind, by
the civilizing effects of indulgence in liberal study." This is
as far back as 1340.

But perhaps the finest specimen of this pious and enlightened liberality, was afforded by the good Bishop of Winches-
ter, William de Wykeham, the munificent founder of New
College, in Oxford. Wood thus expresses himself:—
" Thus was this noble work finished and completed by the
bounty of the thrice worthy and never too much admired
prelate, not so much for the eternizing of his own name, but
chiefly for the public good; that the Holy Writ and all other
sciences might the freer be dilated; that Christ might be
preached, and the true worship of him augmented and sustained; that the number of clerks might be increased, which
were before swept away by pestilences and other miseries of
the world."

That there is a native *vis inertiæ* on the part of the public
in reference to learning, which needs to be operated upon by
aggressive forces from without, and in virtue of which it,
without endowments, and without statutes of apprenticeship,

would speedily decline, is manifest from the whole history of literary institutions. In Fuller's History of Cambridge for 1545, he says, that " there was now a general decay of students, no *colledge* having more scholars therein than hardly those of the foundation, no *volunteers* at all, and only *persons pressed* in a manner by their places to reside; indeed, on the fall of the Abbeys, fell the hearts of all scholars fearing the ruin of learning."

NOTE E. page 59.

The following is a catalogue of those who have been educated at Oxford, and whose names are the most familiar, at least to ourselves, as associated with the learning or the politics of England:—

1. Merton College.—Bishop Jewell, Bishop Hooper, Shute Barrington Bishop of Durham, Duns Scotus, *Wickliffe*, Anthony Wood, Steele.

2. University College.—Thomas Kay or Caius, Lord Herbert, Hurd, Radcliffe, Sir William Jones.

3. Baliol College.—Bishop Douglas, Keil, *Bradley*.

4. Exeter College.—Prideaux, Conybeare, Secker, Lord Shaftesbury, Maundrell, Kennicott.

5. Oriel College.—*Bishop Butler*, Sir Walter Raleigh, Dr. Joseph Wharton.

6. Queen's College.—Henry V. *Bernard Gilpin*, William Gilpin (on the Picturesque), Wingate, Wycherley, Mill (Prolegomena), Halley, *Addison*, Tickell, Seed, Shaw (Travels, &c.), Collins (Poet), Burn (Justice of the Peace).

7. New College.—*Lowth*, *Young*, Pitt (Poet).

8. Lincoln College.—Archbishop Potter, Tindal (Deist), Hervey (Meditations), Wesley.

9. All Souls' College.—*Sir Christopher Wren, Jeremy Taylor, Blackstone*.

10. Magdalene College.—Bishop Horne, Wolsey, Hamp-

den, Hammond, Sacherevell, Yalden (Poet), *Gibbon*, Chandler.

11. Brazen Nose College.—Fox (Martyrs), Buxton (Melancholy), Petty (Political Arithmetic).

12. Corpus Christi College.—Pococke (Traveller), Twyne, *Hooker*, Dr. Nathaniel Foster, Day, Sir Ashton Lever.

13. Christ Church.—*John Owen*, Atterbury, Horsley, Lord Littleton, Lord Mansfield, Ben Jonson, Otway, Gilbert West, Cambden, Gunter, William Penn, Desaguliers, Lord Bolingbroke.

14. Trinity College.—Chillingworth, Denham (Poet), Blount (Traveller), Harrington (Oceana), Derham, Whitby, *Lord Chatham*, Thomas Warton.

15. St. John's College.—Archbishop Laud, Briggs, Sir John Marsham (Chronologist), Josiah Tucker.

16. Jesus College.—Usher.

17. Wadham College.—Walsh (Poet), Admiral Blake, Creech (Lucretius), Dr. Mayow, Harris (Hermes).

18. Pembroke College.—Bishop Bonner, Pym, Whitfield, Shenstone, *Dr. Johnson*.

19. Worcester College.—Sir Kenelm Digby.

20. Hertford College.—Richard Newton, Selden, Dr. Donne, *Charles-Fox*.

21. St. Alban's Hall.—Massinger (Dramatic Poet).

22. Edmund Hall.—Sir Richard Blackmore.

23. St. Mary's Hall.—Sir Thomas More, Harriot.

24. New Inn Hall.—Scott (Christian Life).

25. St. Mary Magdalene Hall.—Sir Henry Vane, Lord Clarendon, Sir Matthew Hale, Theophilus Gale.

The following is a similar list of names associated with Cambridge. The same individual is sometimes connected with both universities; and it will be observed, that Cambridge, on the whole, exceeds Oxford in the number and higher literary stature of its gigantic men:—

1. Peter's House, or College.—Law, Bishop of Carlisle, Dr. Sherlock Senior, Garth the Poet, Gray the Poet.

2. Clarehall.—*Archbishop Tillotson, Cudworth,* Langhorne, Dodd.

3. Pembroke Hall.—Dr. Calamy, *Spencer* (Poet), Mason, *William Pitt.*

4. Granville and Caius College.—*Jeremy Taylor,* Titus Oates, *Dr. Harvey* (Circulation of the Blood), *Dr. Clarke,* Lord Thurlow.

5. Trinity Hall.—Dr. Horsley.

6. Corpus Christi, or Benet College.—Dr. Briggs, Fletcher the Dramatic Poet, Dr. Sykes.

7. King's College.—Pearson (on the Creed), Oughtred, Gouge, Walsingham, Waller, Collins the Free-thinker, Sir Robert Walpole, Horace Walpole.

8. Queen's College.—Bishop Patrick, Erasmus, *Wallis,* Thomas Fuller.

9. Catharine Hall.—Lightfoot (Hebrew), Dr. Sherlock Junior, Hoadley, Reay.

10. Jesus' College.—Archbishop Cranmer, Elliot the Missionary, Flamstead, Fenton, Jortin, Hartley, Sterne, Gilbert Wakefield, Henry Venn.

11. Christ's College.—Latimer, Bishop Porteous, MILTON, Joseph Mede, Francis Quarles, Howe, Sanderson, *Paley.*

12. St. John's College.—Gauden, *Stillingfleet,* Roger Ascham, Cecil Lord Burleigh, Ben Jonson, Otway, Cave, Prior, *Bentley,* Ambrose Philips, John and Thomas Balguy, Ogden, Soame Jenyns, Theophilus Lindsey, Horne Tooke, Churchill.

13. Magdalene College.—Waterland, Lord Stafford, *Waring.*

14. Trinity College.—Wilkins, *Barrow,* Smith (Optics), Tunstall, Newton (Prophecies), Bishop Watson, BACON, NEWTON, *Dryden,* Lord Essex, Donne, *Coke,* Cowley, Pell, Cotes, Conyers Middleton, Atwood, Maskelyne, *Porson.*

15. Emanuel College.—Farmer (Shakespeare), Bishop Hall, Chandler, Hurd, Horrox, *Matthew Poole,* Charnock, Sir William Temple, Law (Serious Call), Martyn (Botany).

16. Sidney Sussex.—Ward (Mathematics), *Oliver Cromwell*, Wollaston.

Beside these, Cambridge can lay claim to *Lord Byron*.

NOTE F. page 75.

The practice of an initial examination obtains in colleges of more recent formation. It does so at the college of Belfast. Those who attend there with a view to the presbyterian ministry, have to undergo examination by a committee of clergymen of their own denomination, previous to their admission as students. At Maynooth they require a pretty high preliminary education; and the common age of their students on entry is seventeen. The following is extracted from the Minutes of Evidence taken by the Commissioners of Inquiry upon Irish Education:—

" It appears, that in order to be admitted into the lowest class, a young man must be able to construe Cæsar's Commentaries, the Works of Sallust, Virgil's Eclogues, and the first four books of the Æneid, Horace's Epistles, and Cicero's Orations against Cataline. He must also be conversant with the Greek Grammar, and he must be able to read the gospel of St. John, the first book of Lucian's Dialogues, and the first three books of Xenophon's Cyropædia? He is liable to be examined in all these books.

" Can you state what would be the probable expense that a young man must have incurred in his education, previous to his admission into that class? I should think they are generally three years at a Latin and Greek school.

" What is the general price of instruction at such a school as they must attend? The general price of instruction in such schools at present, is a guinea a quarter; but as the schools are not numerous in this country, the young men that go to school, or rather their parents, are obliged, in many instances, not only to defray the expenses incurred with the schoolmaster, but likewise to pay for their diet and lodging, very frequently at a considerable distance from the residence of their parents.

" Is the expense of the education which it is necessary to obtain, previously to a young man's being admitted to Maynooth, so great as to make it impossible for persons of a very low order in society to be admitted into the college at Maynooth?   I think it is: and more particularly the expenses they are subjected to on entering, and after entering the college."

It appears, then, from this extract of the Maynooth Evidence, that to obtain the requisite preliminary education, parents have often to send their sons to provincial schools at a considerable distance from home; and that the expense incurred thereby is such, as to place the college education above the reach and ability of the lowest orders.   Notwithstanding, the institution is attended by 391 students; and this is deemed so full an attendance, by the President, Dr. Crotty, that he thinks it would be very inconvenient to have a greater number in one establishment.   There is, therefore, a two-fold instruction in this passage.   First, though our parochial schools should not afford the education required under a new system of regulation for our universities; yet, if there should be one adequate school in each county, for example, we need not wait for a regeneration of an elementary system of scholarship over the whole country, ere we exact a high preliminary education for colleges.   And secondly, we need not despair, notwithstanding the additional expense that would be thus incurred, of a sufficient attendance for the supply of all our learned professions.   The attendance would be somewhat reduced certainly; but the present state of the competition for vacancies in the church, or for employment in the professions of medicine and law, may well convince us, that there is very great room for such a reduction.

The following resolution, therefore, by the Trustees of the Maynooth college, we hold to be worthy of adoption by the colleges of Scotland.

" At a meeting of the Trustees of the Roman Catholic college, held in said college, on the 26th June, 1821, it was unanimously resolved, ' That after the expiration of two years from this date, no scholar shall be admitted upon the establishment of the Royal College of Maynooth who shall not be found capable of answering in the Latin and Greek authors set down in the following entrance course.' "

For the list of books, see the Eight Report on Education in Ireland, page 57.

NOTE G. page 88.

A very effective method of teaching a class, is to prescribe an order of reading to the students, from the best treatises which have been written on the subject taught; and to follow up this reading by a strict daily examination on the part of the Professor. By means of his own running commentary, he can at the same time give his own independent views, and give the colour of his own mind to every successive topic which shall present itself in the course of the session. Between their careful perusal of the best standard works in their own apartments, and their animated converse on the subjects of these with the Professor in his class-room, there is the best security that can be conceived for the students making a sound and well ascertained progress in the various branches of learning. By this method of teaching, the Professor is dispensed from the ponderous and often unnecessary task of composing a full system of lectures. But it does not supersede occasional or supplementary lectures, by which he might rectify, or illustrate, or add, to the lessons of those writers who have gone before him. He might himself, in this way, reach the press through the medium of the chair, and bequeath so many text-books for the courses of philosophy in future generations. It is thus, that we may best realize the twofold advantage of retaining in our colleges all that is most precious in the wisdom and learning of the times that are past, and yet of keeping pace with the most recent discoveries, nay of accelerating their progress.

Note H. page 107.

We trust that, in the department of medicine at least, the London university may have virtually the benefit of a statute of apprenticeship. The statute that none shall obtain license to act as a practitioner who has not attended *a* course of lectures on certain branches of medical learning, goes a great way to secure this benefit for *the* courses that are best fitted to accomplish the candidates for reputation and employment in this honourable profession. We are further hopeful, that even without any statute, this latter motive will operate powerfully in gaining a numerous attendance from the students of law. We have less fear, therefore, of a copious supply of students, on the event of good appointments, for the appropriate classes of two of the learned professions. But while it was well, we think, to refrain from the institution of a theological professorship in the university itself, we feel strongly impressed with the benefits that might result from a certain arrangement which we shall now explain, both to the character of this great metropolitan seminary, and to the interests of theological education.

The friends of the dissenting academies in England will not deny the struggles and the severe efforts which it costs to uphold these establishments. Would it not greatly abridge the expense of them, if relieved altogether from the charge of their student's literary education, they could appropriate their funds to that part of the tuition which was purely theological? This might be accomplished by any body of dissenters, who shall ordain a course of attendance on certain classes of the London university as indispensable for the admission of students into their theological seminary.

Such an act as this must of course be liable to revocation, and would be revoked, on serious offence being taken with the spirit or substance of the instructions in London.

This scheme, so far as it could be proceeded in, we hold to be pregnant with advantages. In the first place, it might secure for the university a statute of apprenticeship of very wide operation. Should half the dissenters of England be thus associated with that institution, a very large yearly supply of students would thence be afforded; and in the security of their attendance, there might be as lofty and sustained a learning upheld as in the endowed colleges of Scotland or England.

But, secondly, it would operate in raising the theological as well as the literary education of the dissenting ministers. When released from every other charge beside that of their divinity classes, they could perfect and extend these nurseries of sacred science, so as to fill their churches with more accomplished theologians.

And, lastly, when regarded in this connection, the London university might become an engine of great moral power; and the oldest and wealthiest establishments of our land might be made to feel its ascendant influence, and be thereby provoked to a most wholesome jealousy. We have adverted, in the text, to the likelihood of its beneficial re-action on the universities of Oxford and Cambridge. But should it, further, be the mean of overspreading England with a lettered and enlightened dissenting ministry, who added the weight of piety to the weight of cultivated talent, we scarcely can imagine how a more powerful, and at the same time a more salutary stimulant could be brought to bear upon the church. We should not apprehend, in such a state of things, the most distant tendency to an overthrow of that venerable hierarchy. But we should certainly look under heaven for its great and glorious revival—and should the London university be really, however indirectly, the cause of a more virtuous ecclesiastical patronage in that country, this, though it meaneth not so, will be its noblest achievement in the cause of humanity and patriotism.

It is on these grounds that we should rejoice in observing such a connection as we have now pointed out between the London university, and the dissenting bodies of England.*

---

* We are glad to observe, in the very intelligent address of the Rev. H. F. Burder, at the opening of Highbury College, a seminary for the education of independent ministers, that he holds out a prospective view somewhat similar to that which we have now given. We do not altogether sympathize with his reflection on the exclusiveness of " a dominant hierarchy." But we join most heartily in his prayer—" May that university which is about to be established in our great metropolis realize the hopes of its best friends and most enlightened advocates! May it afford the most valuable facilities for laying deep and broad that foundation of literature and science, on which our theological seminaries may erect a superstructure fair and firm."

In the report of the Committee for 1826, on the college at Homerton, there occur the following extracts, which an intelligent reader will at once perceive as bearing upon this question.

" It becomes necessary for your Committee to direct the attention of the Meeting to the serious diminution which has taken place in the annual receipts, arising in part from the distressing reduction in the list of subscribers, occasioned by death and the extraordinary commercial calamities which have so widely affected the general interests of society, and partly from its having been found necessary, in order finally to close the Building account, and to liquidate the balance due to the late Treasurer, to sell out £1000, 3 per cent. Red. and £105 new 4 per cent.

" By this indispensable measure, coupled with the sale of stock in the preceding year, the permanent revenue of the Society is diminished nearly £100 per annum ; and an inspection of the Treasurer's accounts will show that the annual expenditure exceeds the entire income by at least £350, an excess which must lead to most ruinous consequences unless repaired by measures of a vigorous and instantaneous character. To such measures your Committee pledge themselves, and most earnestly entreat all the friends of the Institution to co-operate with them, by strenuous exertions to procure donations and annual subscriptions to such an extent as can alone perpetuate the benefits which this Society has been enabled to confer upon the Churches during the last hundred years.

" The object of the Institution, which has existed about a hundred years, is to support twenty young men of decided and approved piety, who possess respectable talents, and are desirous of devoting themselves to the glory of God, and the immortal welfare of mankind, by engaging in the work of the Christian ministry, in pursuing a course of study adapted to the attainment of such branches of literature as may best qualify them for the intelligent and honourable discharge of the sacred office to which they aspire. The period of time allotted to the entire course is six years; the first two of which are occupied solely in classical pursuits, and the remaining four in classical, theological, and philosophical studies. *In cases where a classical education has been previously enjoyed, the term of study is contracted proportionably to the attainments which have been made.*"

Note I. page 111.

The melancholy effect of leaving religious instruction to be originated by the native and spontaneous demand of the people, is most strikingly exemplified in the southern and western sections of the United States of America. The following extract is from the narrative of a Tour by the Rev. Samuel J. Mills through that country.

" Never will the impression be erased from our hearts, that has been made by beholding those scenes of wide-spreading desolation. The whole country, from Lake Erie to the Gulph of Mexico, is as the valley of the shadow of death. Darkness rests upon it. Only here and there, a few rays of gospel light pierce through the awful gloom. This vast country contains more than a million of inhabitants. Their number is every year increased, by a mighty flood of emigration. Soon they will be as the sands on the sea-shore for multitude. Yet there are at present only a little more than one hundred Presbyterian or Congregational ministers in it. Were these ministers equally distributed throughout the country, there would be only one to every ten thousand people. But now there are districts of country, containing from twenty to fifty thousand inhabitants entirely destitute. ' And how shall they hear without a preacher ?' "

Note K. page 120.

The excellent Philip Henry, who was expelled from his charge as the established minister of a parish for nonconformity, had the opportunity of contrasting the comparative efficiency of the two systems. We hold the following testimony from him to be peculiarly valuable.

" Yet the opportunity he found there was of doing the more good, by having those that were his charge near about him, made him all his days bear his testimony to parish order, where it may be had upon good terms, as much more eligible, and more likely to answer the end, than the congregational way of gathering churches from places far distant, which could not ordinarily meet to worship God together. From this experience here, though he would say we must do what we can, when we cannot do what we would, he often wished and prayed for the opening of a door, by which to return to that order again."

See the edition of Philip Henry's Life, by J. B. Williams, page 47. There is a note subjoined to this extract, by the present, or some former Editor, by which it is attempted, but without success, to neutralize the force of this important testimony. I may here take the opportunity of adding, that this edition by Mr. Williams contains much original matter, whereby he has enhanced still more the value of one of the most precious religious biographies in our language.

NOTE L. page 128.

In the short but very instructive pamphlet of my enlightened friend Mr. Hale of Homerton, entitled, " Cursory Remarks upon the Present State of Protestant Dissenting Congregations," we meet with ample confirmation of our principles on this subject. He, though himself a zealous dissenter, and a most liberal supporter of their interests, seems to feel that these interests can only be upheld by a severe struggle against the popular and the prevailing bias of our nature. The following observations by Mr. Hale we deem to be in the highest degree important and judicious.

" In the common transactions and business of life, we know that an increased demand for any of its comforts or luxuries will always secure an increased supply; but we must proceed in an inverse ratio, when it regards the welfare of immortal souls. ' The carnal mind is enmity against God.' There is no desire in the human race for religious instruction —they are totally averse from it; and, to speak in the political language just referred to, we must always overstock the market with a supply before we can have reason to expect any demand."—

" There are many worthy pastors in various parts of the empire, who know, from bitter experience, the truth of these observations; who have been struggling for years against the tide of adversity, and whose extreme distresses are known only to the afflicted partners of their lives, and to those of their children who have been early inured to the severe privation of almost every domestic comfort. Their anguish has often been such as to render them totally unfit for the labours of the Sabbath : and while they have been called to exhort their congregation to the practical exercise of every relative duty, they have been sensible that their own inability to discharge their just debts has been too freely circulated by some of their hearers; that unjust motives have been partially ascribed to their conduct, and that thus an advantage is taken, by the enemies of religion, to destroy the effects of their preaching.

" I am aware that it will be said by some, that the young Minister should endeavour to keep a school; but this is not desirable. The constant and faithful discharge of his ministerial duties will sufficiently occupy his time, while any other employment will naturally tend to diminish his usefulness. In many situations the establishment of a school is not practicable; in others the ground is already so occupied that the attempt would be fruitless; and frequently, where Ministers have for a while persevered in the plan, it has ended in their failure, and sometimes in the abandonment of their pastoral duties."—

" It must, however, be admitted, ' that there are many ministers of irreproachable character at this time unable to obtain pastoral engagements; and also, that there are many stations highly interesting and important that are suffering greatly from the want of able and learned ministers."—

" What must be the feelings of a young man who has devoted himself to the Christian ministry, and who, by his amiable conduct and persevering industry while in the college, has gained the approbation and affection of his tutors —I say, what must be the feelings of this holy young man, when, after preaching acceptably to the congregation which he has been supplying, and from which he has received a pressing invitation to become their pastor, he finds, to his inexpressible grief, that the income which they have been accustomed to give to their minister will not be sufficient for his bare maintenance !"

" With respect to those ' stations, exceedingly interesting and important, which are suffering incalculably from the want of Ministers,' it is acknowledged, that the chief obstacle to such stations, being suited with able Pastors, is the not raising a sufficient provision for their frugal maintenance."—

" By far the greater part of our dissenting congregations lie under the charge of not contributing what they ought to do for their Pastors."*

NOTE M. page 156.

The Crown, in its church patronage of Scotland, has been in the habit of evincing so far a deference to the wishes of those who are interested in its nominations, as generally

---

* The Pamphlet from which these extracts have been taken, was called forth by the following observation of a writer in the Congregational Magazine, who seems to have felt, and to have felt truly, the feebleness of the native demand for the services of ministers:—

" When the supply of any article exceeds the demand, the invariable consequence is, a diminutiou of its value. If ministers should increase in a much greater ratio than the necessities of the churches require, the inevitable consequence will be, a degradation of the ministerial character."

to decide the appointment by the wishes of the majority of landed proprietors in the parish—estimating that majority, however, by the valued rent. We should deem it an improvement on the practice, were Government, in this matter, to grant the benefice on the application of the numerical majority of heritors. Should the elders be admitted along with the heritors to a voice in the application, this would place the Crown Patronages of Scotland on the same footing which obtained in regard to all the patronages at the beginning of the last century. For ourselves, we are not very confident that a purer exercise of the right would be secured by any further extension of the franchise.

Historically, a universal suffrage in the appointment of clergymen has not proved itself to be a specific against the evil of corrupt and unworthy nominations. The Unitarianism which has taken possession of many of the originally orthodox chapels in England; and the Arianism which entered the Presbyterian Synod of Ulster in Ireland, sprung up there under a system of popular election. It is true that Arianism is now rapidly declining in the North of Ireland—and that, too, because of the recent nominations being almost all in favour of orthodox clergymen. But this is saying no more for patronage as vested in the people, than that it is partaking in the improvement which is now taking place in the exercise of all other patronage. The dominant spirit of the country is fast working its way throughout all the forms and frameworks of outward constitution.

While upon this subject, we may take the opportunity of expressing our regret that the Government Grant has not been sooner restored to the college of Belfast—and that, too, from the apprehension of its proving a nursery of Arianism. Even though it were greatly worse in this respect than it is at present, we should have no such fear—being assured that in the growing orthodoxy of the synod of Ulster, and in the necessary influence which, apart altogether from stipulations, that body must have on the professorial appointments, there is a moral security against the apprehended evil, far greater than could be provided by any formal ratifications.

ERRATA.

Page 161, line 22, *for* exertion *read* erection.
    162,   1, *for* there *read* their.
    163,   10, *for* found *read* feared.
    167,   10, *for* have *read* lose.

FINIS.